POETRY NOW

GROWING OLD

1993

Edited by Veronica Hannon

First published in Great Britain in 1993 by
POETRY NOW
1-2 Wainman Road, Woodston,
Peterborough, PE2 7BU

Foreword

I am only in my twenties so the editing of this collection was something of a challenge - I must admit that I approached the poems with a predetermined idea of what the content would be like. From our youngest years the term 'generation gap' has been bounded around. After the first couple of poems this term became irrelevant as I settled back to enjoy them. I was given the privilege of seeing behind the dates on the birth certificates that defines which generation of society you belong to. More so than most collections of verse I was once again struck at the power of poetry: the pure communication of joys, hopes and fears. This collection is full of that power. Each has a strong and individual voice that lifts it above any age.

The poetry we received had such a depth of commitment and such an important comment to make on the world in which we live that it soon became obvious what an important and relevant book it would be both for today and the future: it is ageless.

Contents

Sour Charity	Margaret Cox	1
Age: Old	Michel Joseph Smith	2
Born Again me	Joy Griffiths	3
De Profundis Mk 3	B Devereux	4
Jetsam	W L Weaver	5
Untitled	Ralph Morgan	6
Time	Pamela Swanson	7
Eventide Home	Eileen Plume	9
When I Grow Old	Janet Lomax	10
Parents' Prayer	Arthur Douglas Russell	11
Time	Trevor Daintith	12
Untitled	Elizabeth Lucas Harrison	13
At Bay	Thelma James	14
Compensations	Daphne Webb	15
The Thickening of a Sportsman's Blood	Lewis Coles	16
Aspects	Emma Millman	17
The Sands of Time	Hugh Eastman	18
The Last Horizon	T W Alsop	20
A Fine Disguise	Stephanie Gifford	21
Old Man	Eric Nixon	22
Eighty	Michael Davidson	23
It's No Joke	Nancy Holt	24
Untitled	M Wilson	25
Old Dried Apricot Faces	Len Landers	26
In Retirement	L K Lawler	27
Second Thoughts on my Parents	Christopher Bowyer	28
Growing Old	Pat Knight	29
Lament of a Retired Lady Gardener	Joan White	30
Progression	Elaine Marlow	31
Old	Barbara Middlestorb	32
Trains on Time	Chris Rogers	33
The Railway Man	Brian L Heap	34
Grandma's Footsteps	Jenny Johns	36

Stretching Out	Helen Allison	37
Not Ready Yet	Dorothy Will	38
Time	Barbara Wedgewood	39
Growing Old	Grace Williams	40
The Lesson	Linda Marshall	41
Past all That	Stephen N Mackinnon	42
Senile Mother	Anne McAleavy	43
Unspoken Thoughts	Victor Green	44
Requiem for Spring	Jess Chambers	45
Growing Old	I Taylor	46
Disbelief	Maureen Harper	47
The Salesman	Heather Wastie	48
A New Visitor to the Home	Ruth Wallace	49
Only Half Their Age	Pamm Morris	50
Winds of Life	Jean Collins	51
Architect's Report	Olga Townend	52
Here is the Work	David Orman	53
Every Ten Years	Margaret Morley	54
With Age	Elizabeth J Hargreaves	55
Old - but Snappy!	Betty Skipper	56
Too Kind	Margaret Williams	57
Homing	Jean Froggett	58
Tree Cycles	Iain McDaniel	59
Untitled	Gwynneth der Parthog	60
Futures	Pamela Sinclair	61
Never a Grandmother	Greeba Brydges-Jones	62
The Waiting	Margaret McDougall	63
These Hands	Brenda Barry	64
Time Passing	Isla Elliott	65
Untitled	Peggy Leng	66
Survival	Pat Rigg	67
The Choice	Grace Graham	68
Now That I am Seventy-Five	Eric Oates	69
We are Mere Tenants in This Spinning World	Angela Platt	70
Looking Ahead	June Gerrish	71
Does Growing Old Improve With Age?	Sheila Fermor Clarkson	72

The Time Barrier	Michael Owers	73
Barefooting	Valerie English	74
Old Age	Leslie Ratcliff	75
Sonnet on Old Age	Brian Gee	76
Will was Right	L Brewer	77
In the Event of my Death Abroad	Gerald Watkin	78
The Resolution	Jean Shaw	79
Ballad of a Grateful Woman	Ann Redcliff	80
A Rueful Rhyme	Anne L Haines	81
Alas for Old Age!	Iris Allingham	82
Loneliness	Stephanie Batstone	83
Rôle Play	Judy Barrett	84
Why go for the Gold	Trish Kelly	85
Diagnosis - MS	Barbara Murray	86
Growing Old	Gladys Dixon	87
Growing Old Gracefully	Lynda Forbes Jones	88
Internal	Elisabeth Spooner	89
An Age Old Poem	Michele Wolf	90
There is a Hair Growing Out of my Chin	Pam Finch	91
Who Cares?	J Machin	92
Looking Down	Geoffrey Holloway	93
Growing Old	P Homer	94
Tortoise Club	Thora Beddard	95
Autumn	Peter K Broadbent	96
Growing Old	S H B	98
The Warning	C L Shurie	99
The Impossible Dream	D P Glanville	100
Stars Must Know	John Farrell	101
Westerns	Judy Diss	102
Geriatric Ward Chesterton Hospital Cambridge	Brian D Thompson	103
How Did I Come to This?	John Gillespie	104
Mobility	Norman Hurst	106
Untitled	Michael J Erian	107
Untitled	Margaret Harvey	108
Sea Gardens	Peter R Dennis	109

Mirror Image	Mike Devereux	110
Thirty Thousand Nights	John M Rimmer	111
It Happens to the Best of us	Sybil Hurcomb	112
Nursing Home	Pauline Harley	113
On Growing Old	Betty Murray	114
Stillborn	Matthew Porter	115
The 'Plaint of the Unmarried Daughter	Miriam Greenwood	116
Old Age - a Celebration	Ann Mather	118
Viewpoint in Srajevo	Geoffrey Parker-Platt	119
I'm Going to be a Granny!	Jinny Owen	120
The Tourists	Elizabeth Clifton	121
Untitled	Kitty Bould	122
Mid Sixties Sonnet	Patricia Richardson	123
No Fool Like an Old Fool	Ralph Stephenson	124
Alzheimer	Brian Mitchell	125
Reflections	John Clare	126
Untitled	M P Ward	127
Peace	Edna Weaver	128
Old	Jane Cockerham	129
University of the Third Age	Cynthia Manning	130
Thank you for the Days	David J Ayres	131
The Stick People	Mary Bourne Richmond	132
Fair, Fat and Fifty	Gillian Smith	134
Thoughts on Growing Old	Jean P Bidmead	136
The Third Age	Lilian Mantle	137
Nowt	Kenneth Wadsworth	138
The Last Laugh	Elizabeth Stanley	139
I'm Not Sad	Janet Bradley	140
November Men	Stan Dodd	141
Life's Tree	John Redmond	142
Parable	Gerard Owen	143
Regrets	Ann Green	144
In my Third Age	Barbara Dettmer	145
I'm Here	Mo Evans	146
Thoughts of a Geriatric	Roy Hobbs	147
The Woman I Remember	Adrian Cox	148
Old Man in the Library	P Brindle	149

Old Age	Carol Archer	150
Evening At Hove	Michael Irish	151
The Choice	Lewis Coles	152
Untitled	Judith Anne Bedlow	153
Cloud Bound	Helen Buckingham	154
Life Goes on	May Haywood	155
Am I Old?	Yvette M Beaumont	156
Growing Old	Edna Leader	157
Now	Chrisitne Oddy	158
Lethargy	Doreen Fletcher	159
Full Circle	Moyna Broad	160
So Nice	John Hendeles	161
Serene Old Age	Mollie Freeman	162
The Pensioners of England	John Victor Webb	163
Live Slowly	Christopher Rosier	164
Moving on	Angela Lanyon	165
When I'm Old	Rosemary Benzing	166
On the Death of my Father	Roger Bloor	167
Growing . . . Old?	Eve Craig	168
Too Late	June Ansell	169
My Mother	Ann Fogg	170
Plea	Roy E Brownlow	171
To my Children	Jean Margaret Peace	172
The Ebbing Tide	Joan Poynter	173
I'll Never be Ready to Say Goodbye	Freda Ball	174
Farewell to Canutism	Valmai Holt	175
Irrelevant Age	Ruth Hitchings	176
Growing Old	Marguerite Haselton	177
Thicker Knickers	Margaret Foreman	178
On the Death of a Loved One	J A Uttley	179
What Day is it Tomorrow?	Mary Erricker	180
State of the Heart	Gerry McKee	181
Marjorie	Elizabeth Buckman	182
Grandaughter	Betty Kay	183
Last Lap	Dorothy Cowlin	184
Reflections	Nargis Qureshi	185

Going Home	Stuart Crabb	186
No Thanks Methuselah	John Marshman	187
Full of Years	Peter Donaldson	188
Growing Older	E B Steel	189
The Future of Friends	Pat Austin Stone	190
This Retiring Life	Ruth Chapman	191
Keep on Knocking	Jocelyn M Britcher	192
Old Man's Memories	Austin Shorney	193
Growing Old	Josephine Bromley	194
Growing Old	Arthur George Carter	195
A Rest Home (They Say)	Marian Thomas	196

Sour Charity

It's there in the whiff of stale urine in a pair of tweed trousers
The defiant tobacco smoke in a comfortable old jacket
It's where lavender water mingles in a stained nylon dress
Where careful mothballs still guard faded starched cotton sheets
And dusty bags lie unopened with presents inside . . .
The dread stink of leaking old age
And I know as I tighten my pelvis and deep breathe my Chanel
I'd die if it happened to me.

Margaret Cox

Age: Old

I cannot help but feel it,
my senses forever touch it,
each day I see and watch it,
upon my tongue I taste it.

The life I live serves it,
each breath I breathe exhales it,
ambitions gone before it,
I've grown up to despise it.

Michel Joseph Smith

Born Again me

Tonight this rusty busty fusty old body
moved in a dance
I got up from my chair
and as though in a trace
stepped onto the floor, unthinking, alone
as my feet and my legs with wills of their own moved
Yes I moved out of the Granny rust
I shook off the dust and I moved.
I daresay I creaked
and possibly squeaked
but the music was loud
and nobody noticed I limped a bit
as I twisted and danced for the joy of it.
I sang and I smiled and it felt so right
to be doing exactly this tonight.
So much more fitting than sitting and knitting
or watching the box or reading or writing
Oh this was a great deal more exciting
So away with the polish, the duster, the hoover
I'm a born-again me and a great little mover.

Joy Griffiths

De Profundis Mk 3

At present I am feeling quite depressed;
A state of mind at which I wryly grin
These days, for I am nearly at my best,
What with a job and something left for gin.
The thing that almost drives me to the bin
Is having no reserves; in short, the bore
Of making *just* enough to keep the kin.
I'm getting old, and only forty-four.

And then, by God! the landlord, *so* distressed
That everything about his house of tin
Is *not quite working properly.* That pest
(He frankly owns) the tenant, tends to sin
So grievously against him that the thin
And highly-priced amenities he swore
In print were *good* might now be called just *in.*
I'm getting old, and only forty-four.

To cap it all, it seems that Youth's possessed
Uniquely of the Clue; that all its din
And mindlessness add up, while we, the rest -
Absurd, our antithetic Yang and Yin
Unquickened by the lout's adrenaline -
Make plus and minus zero. What's the score?
Does only *now* enlightenment begin?
I'm getting old, and only forty-four.

Envoi
Prince, does *your* daughter go about half-dressed?
Does *your* son bring home what looks like a whore?
Does *your* wife say they shouldn't be repressed?
I'm getting old, and only forty-four.

B Devereux

Jetsam

Red-rimmed from the night's weeping
Her eyes, in their dark sockets
Are hard and hurt and hating.
Seamed flesh hangs from a fragile skull,
Grey wisps of hair fly from a twisted knot,
And clothes, outdated, cover angled bones.
Her clumsy, slippered feet
Shuffle the length of worn linoleum,
Pause at the threshold and - no backward glance -
Step from worn sill;
A whole life severed by the slamming of a door.

She goes, unwilling, to a world of light,
A place of warmth and ease;
A bright, clean, coloured heaven
Full of practised kindness,
Peopled by exiles, banished from the hearth,
Their only crime their age and their infirmity.

W L Weaver

Untitled

Well goodness me, I'm fifty nine,
That is a big surprise,
'Cos I still look more handsome
Than all the other guys.

I'm sure I can't be fifty nine,
I still feel I am twenty,
I still feel young and full of beans,
I've energy in plenty.

It's clear I can't be fifty nine,
No - fifty nine sounds old,
At fifty nine you start to shrink,
And always feel the cold.

I'm not like that, no not at all,
I'm still youthful and fit,
I still like food, I still like wine,
Still chase the girls a bit.

I creak a little here and there,
I can't deny that's true,
A few worn bits to be replaced,
Then I'd be just like new.

Ralph Morgan

Time

breakfast time -
time to move
from bed to chair -
from bed to chair -
the selfsame moves
again again
that you have made
so many times
between the endless hours -

ninety years
to end up here
battling
from chair to bed
from bed to chair
and chair to bed
and bed to chair again -

gradually
you gather force
and stand to step
and step to stand
on crumbling crumbling legs -

the carpet rises
up to eyes
reaching fingers
from the grave -
and you are down
almost alive
like ninety years
of nothing more to claim -

arms from nowhere
pull you up
and place you in
an absent chair -
somewhere a tissue
on your cheek
brushes off the tears.

Pamela Swanson

Eventide Home

Down in the basement they iron the laundry,
Hanging the clothes on racks to air.
On a stifling afternoon in June,
I ironed for three hours there.

Some of their clothes are smart and new,
As if someone did really care,
Others are old, and tired and worn,
(They have been longest there).

Amelia Brown has a loving daughter,
Who calls on her once a week,
But for Joe and Betty, Ernest and Martha
The outlook's pretty bleak.

The children used to look in often
With books, and flowers and buns,
But now 'They've got so much to do!'
And lately no-one comes.

Albert has recently lost The Missus,
He sits in a corner and sighs,
Refusing all comfort - enwrapped in silence,
The tears of a child in his eyes.

As soon as the funeral was decently over
The Family had only one fear -
'Daddy will never be able to cope!
What luck that they took him in here!'

So Albert and Emily, Dora and Ernest,
Sit as the days go by,
Sleeping and eating - eating and sleeping,
And waiting, - just waiting to die.

Eileen Plume

When I Grow Old

When I grow old I'll be content
For life to pass me by.
No pangs of love no heartbreak
And no bitter tears to cry.

When I grow old I'll be upset
To give up squash for bowls,
Or hang about on courses
Knocking balls down little holes.

When I grow old I'll sell my car -
Old eyes do get dimmer.
But what fun to do a ton -
A 'burn up' on me zimmer!

When I grow old I'll sit and dream
Of things that used to be.
But all that's in the future
'Cos I'm only ninety-three!

Janet Lomax

Parents' Prayer

Children, pray be kind enough
- or, maybe, just to mind enough -
to show your love to us,
your too-flawed parents!
Yes, you will suffer
disillusion, as
our moral postures
fade away in Age,
and we cry, and plead
an Armistice,
before your bold
and sceptical
convictions.
So sorry.
And we
will doubtless
fail to measure
up to standards drawn:
Forgive us our trespass,
in your quiet evening vespers.

. . . You see, - perhaps we sought for Truth
as prospectors seek treasure,
and maybe succeeded
in some minor measure.
But gold dust is scarce;
often unseen,
as we glean
what has
been.
God bless.

Arthur Douglas Russell

Time

Filch from consuming Time
Such moments as you may.
The fleeting Present glides
Unchecked upon its way.

The Past in stiffened death
Unalterable lies,
The unborn Future holds
No happy certainties.

Take up what crumbs may be
With hands that yet may hold.
Too soon your grasp will fail
In age's numbing cold.

Trevor Daintith

Untitled

I count the days till I am old
Old and at peace
With memories
Not to hold
But to bequeath

To breathe
With simulated carelessness
And nothing to redeem
The freedom of approaching certainty

To walk
With a faint and ready smile
The last and most enchanting mile
Into the essence of my dream

Elizabeth Lucas Harrison

At Bay

Something glinting
In powdered whiteness.

A bright red gash
Beneath black terror.

An ash blonde frame,
An age-old subject.

Pale watered eyes
Set in masked decay.

Thelma James

Compensations

I hate my hair, I hate my feet
The bit between admits defeat,
Face lines of age will rarely flatter,
Grey hair, false teeth, and glasses matter.

Hours now to pass the time of day
With neighbours, friends, and have my say,
To paint, to sketch, watch Spring anew,
And time to do the crossword too.

Slowing down with memory poorer,
Take tasks singly, making surer,
Cruel advancing years, sad loss of youth
Bow inevitably, mirror shows the truth.

Still, children, theirs too, play their part
I've immortality in children and in art,
No dashing off to work, I sit and sew,
With leisure now, time to watch the flowers grow.

Daphne Webb

The Thickening of a Sportsman's Blood

Are you serious?
This growing old gracefully lark
Is for the birds.
Me, I'm a sportsman (or rather was).
Bruises worn with pride
Were the mark of my virility.
But now: now I'm surrounded
By intimations of mortality.

Varicose Veins!
You'd think I'd been a bloody
Shop assistant.
When I was young I revelled
In the hard knocks;
They were proof of my eternal manhood.
But now; now I worry
About the thickening of my blood.

Think of the good times?
Well, thanks for the advice,
I wish I could.
People say 'Oh look!' 'Remember him?'
'What a star!'
What does it matter? It's only talk.
Now; now I'm arthritic
And can hardly walk.

So tell me doctor -
You've given me so many tablets;
Can't you slip in a couple more,
A cure for old age, once and for all?

Lewis Coles

Aspects

Age; leaves passion's sting behind.
But deeper love, the soul, does bind
around, with ties of given grace
from battles won, but not against age.
Let not sorrow nestle, for fleet footed youth,
'tis, but a twilight for tomorrow's dawn
where life's, bitter sweet Balm, tends aid to soothe
the profound felt pain of anothers youth,
and the veil of fear of approaching age
does part, to show a different view,
For; you see yourself in a daughters face
and bless, good-fortune that has gifted you
the love, that was born of your own young days
and, passing years, in warm content, you, do gently swathe.

Emma Millman

The Sands of Time

The sands of time are running out!
I'm short of breath and prone to gout;
Blood pressure rises ever higher,
I may explode as I expire.

My hair is now completely white,
What's left of it, and, every night,
I get up twice for you know what,
My waterworks have gone to pot.

I've joints that creak, and teeth I keep
Beside the bed while I'm asleep.
No longer nature's master plan,
But Shakespeare's seventh age of man.

But, if my life is less than bliss,
Perhaps you should remember this
Before you put me in my shroud -
The silver lining to my cloud.

When my white hairs require a trim
It's done half price: when eyesight dim
Demands a boost to help me see
The state helps out this OAP.

Rail Rover cards can let me roam
Quite cheaply miles and miles from home.
While stately homes, and theatres, too,
They let me in for less than you.

All sorts of people now connive
To help me since I'm sixty five.
It is my age I have to thank
For money mounting in the bank.

But, sometimes, as the loot I stash,
I wonder 'What's the use of cash
With nothing left to spend it on?
No wine, no women, and no song!'

Hugh Eastman

The Last Horizon

Slippers shuffle to my doorway
Squat figure peers in from the gloom
Looks to see that all is tidy
Put away within the room

From her working days now distant
In charge with searching peering eyes
To check the cleaning's done properly
Still she wants to supervise

Now, another, taller figure
'Come on Ethel - with me please'
Guides away the silent roamer
With Alkzheimers brain disease

Past my doorway now like a rag doll
Lies shrunken figure in a chair
To the lounge she goes unknowing
Where she left or when she's there

No emotions, no decisions
For some it's every day the same
Quality of life so lacking.
Cabbages in all but name

Thankfully I've all my marbles
But failing heart and short of breath
Nursing Home the last confinement
Patiently awaiting death

Silver hair an outward symbol
Of faculties now getting old
Frailty that's so frustrating
To the memories of gold

T W Alsop

A Fine Disguise

She goes about in disguise, this girl:
Grey wig, thick spectacles, a pensioner's white mac.
But really she's a fat fourteener,
Ready to giggle and giggle,
Eating too many Mars bars and forever falling in love.

But really she's a tiny child with curly hair,
Fondling a polished conker,
Scuffling her feet through fallen leaves -
'Hi, Granny!' yell the passing yobbos.
Who's that, she wonders. Me?

But really she's thirtyish, tanned, travelled,
Stepping into a pizzeria for lunch.
The waitress stares. 'You want a cup of tea or something?'

Out in the street, she sees, edging towards her,
A quaint old bird with specs and spiky hair -
Heavens! Herself, in a shop window.
'Ah well, a fine disguise. It even took in me!'

Stephanie Gifford

Old Man

Sitting amongst his cares
in a lonely room,
long overgrown with time,
he turns the pages of his mind,
and breathes the cerements of days
which wind among his memories.
Faces he knew are mixed with dreams;
he wears a life composed by time
which comes and goes within his mind.
He moves among his empty chairs,
silent in the evening gloom,
shuffling in his mental tomb
the cards of time he used to play.
No longer able to be fair
he cheats himself in several ways.

Eric Nixon

Eighty

Unreconciled for sixty years
She reads the faded card Jim signed
Still hoping Flanders' field
Would someday send him home.

Her grandson in Australia might ring.
His father died at Anzio,
Not quite the foreign field
Beloved by Rupert Brooke.

The vicar asks about her fading eyes.
You're on the waiting list?
He talks in reminiscent tones
About how Jesus loves us all
The crosses we must bear,
Imparts a blessing hastily.

The social sent her forms
About allowances, entitlements
And what to do if destitute
Warned against untruths
Date as postmark, confidential
State your age and ethnic origin.

'They must be mad, I've been here sixty years'
She whispered as she read.

So for a joke, she wrote
A hundred, darkest Africa,
They took her at her word
And sent encyclopaedic documents
In languages she could not understand.

She had a drink or two - and more
Then fell asleep and missed her grandson's call.

Michael Davidson

It's No Joke

We all want to grow old with grace
Slowing down our normal pace
Trying not to mind at all
The aching joints, the failing sight,
The rising several times a night,
And memory gone beyond recall.
Some I know have met with humour
Even the suspicion of a tumour
Yet it isn't always easy to treat longevity
With levity.

Loss of partner, husband, wife
Calls for a fresh start in life.
Weep in secret. Do not moan.
We visit friends to laugh and chatter
About things that do not matter
'Come to tea and have a natter,
Can't be much fun on your own.'
'Bridge (or Scrabble) will be jolly,
Sandwich lunch first from the trolley
I've invited Peg and Molly.'
Friendly voices on the 'phone.
'Thanks so much, it's been such fun!
Goodbye, goodbye then everyone!'
Then home to empty house alone.
No, it isn't always easy to treat with levity
Longevity.

Nancy Holt

Untitled

Last night I lay in your arms
And the firelight was tender to us.
You gave such pleasure that I worshipped you
The ageless touch of skin on skin
When all reserves are set aside
And two alone together make what they may.
The quick strong thrusts to fill the aching yearning
And afterwards, the firelight, gently flickering.

Such joys are for the young, they say
So have our six score years, and more
Renewed the right to pass this joyous door
Or was that key not lost, just laid aside?

M Wilson

Old Dried Apricot Faces

Old, dried apricot faces.
Torturing frames.

Buying fruit.
Worms in their bags.

Arguing old currency.
Shopping at laughtermongers.

Delaying traffic.

Squatting on piles.

Rain in their eyes,
Dripping years.

In transit.
Handled with care.
Dropped.

Holding children across roads.
Smiling.

Manoeuvring flagstones,
Visiting heirs.

The Old Grand Piano.

Tinkering tunes.
Moths in the felt.

Len Landers

In Retirement

Assuming mistakenly cause and effect to have meaning
He aspired to a political career,
But when the price of this became too dear
He discovered in himself a leaning

Towards honest journalism - which was silly,
For facts were not what people wished to know.
Sub-editors were savage; willy-nilly
He came to think it time for him to go.

At last, much later on, he found the garden;
He loiters easily green paths along,
And has no doubt at all that he did wrong

As, whistling lively tunes, he hopes for pardon -
A lifer whom remission has set free,
He notices the foxglove fit the bee.

L K Lawler

Second Thoughts on my Parents

Now that I'm as old as you will ever be
Surely it's time that I should know you as you were,
Not blinded by the ache of love and pity,
But as a stranger might, weighing good and bad,
Kindly, the better to forgive or understand.

Yet something still rebels as if it were immoral.
If that is so, then what of other judgements made
Where intelligence is free in an unimpeded mind,
Are they, perhaps, for lack of love, more staring blind?

Christopher Bowyer

Growing Old

I used to look at old people
Through unknowing eyes.
Never imagining that one day
I would be there too.
The loss of youth affects every aspect
Of life.
Retirement, ailments, the prospect of impending death.
No paid job represents loss of structure -
In its place comes time-filling 'til the end.
Keep-fit classes, badminton, outings
With the 'white-cardi brigade', over sixties clubs,
Holidays if finances and friends are available.
There is time, time, always time
Yet little fulfilment.
There is isolation, loneliness and selfishness
If family or friends have not been cultivated
During young and middle-aged days.
The old are left and regarded as a nuisance
When baby sitting, child-minding days are over.
They are left to seek outside contacts
Otherwise little stimulus enters the home.
Pets, books, radio, television, hobbies
All have their place in the day.
Yet
The emptiness, the not being needed, no one-to-one closeness
The 'What shall we do with mother?,'
The 'Whose turn is it to have her at Christmas?'
Growing old is a frightening, unsatisfactory, helpless
Time of life.
Death may be a welcome release.

Pat Knight

Lament of a Retired Lady Gardener

At age sixty five now I've had to retire;
A gardener I need but too dear to hire.

I love my garden - I find it relaxing -
But the older I get it's all much too taxing.
My lawn's in a mess, I've two fairy rings;
Wisley have told me what trouble that brings.

It's hard work you know (the paths need cleaning),
I'm all on the go (the butts are leaning).
I'm getting disheartened (the shed is slipping),
I need my tools sharpened (the Yew needs clipping).

Gardening books - I've read every one;
And TV programmes make it such fun.
I'd love a garden that's easy to do,
Have friends to tea, admiring the view.

From this tale of woe I think you'll agree
That I now need a toy-boy to come and help me!

Joan White

Progression

Am I becoming a person to be put up with?
Oh yes, I still work but even if they cared
I can't discuss that.
Eyes are raised to heaven at my attempts to be interesting,
(I should recognise this sign having once
Achieved perfection in it myself.)
Lively questions are out as this is prying,
So trivia remains, the garden, even the weather!
Soon they'll be telling their friends
They took me for a drive last Sunday.

Elaine Marlow

Old

birth
and death
reasons for celebration
but neither was *my* choice

growth
consists of
joy and pain
but leads to peace

ageing
with its
wonderful high points
but inevitable nadir

old
is a
state of mind -
oh, and of body

Barbara Middlestorb

Trains on Time

How gentle were those days of steam,
How long the journey ahead did seem,
And even when the diesel came
We appeared to trundle on the same;
Then middle-age (the thoughtless swine)
Arrived to electrify the line.

Chris Rogers

The Railway Man

For forty years he'd buffed and cleaned great engines'
brass until it gleamed
On engine footplate, firstly steam, then on to Kenya's
long sought dream
Of monsters painted blue and grey - Kenya's diesel
powered railway.

Remembers miles in sun and rain, through valley, hill
and endless plain.
Hypnotic, lonely, single, line serving the people, farm
and mine,
Sped on many a hot clear day on a train of Kenya's railway.

His wives now dead, the years have flown, his village now
no longer home;
Small pension, long commuted, gone, four daughters sold and
not one son.
For living now to beg and pray, retired from Kenya's rich
railway.

Nairobi, 'water from the spring', whose praise 'developed'
nations sing.
Metropolis modern and slick, with skyrise lifts that often stick,
Connects with places miles away, by Kenya's wide spread railway.

A wide road with polluted airs from multitudes of rushing cars,
Into the city from high ridge passes over a hump backed bridge
Standing guard over the cleared way of Kenya's pride, the old
railway.

Under that bridge he slept and ate, his days spent on the parapet
Watching traffic pushing, rushing, and the trains, important,
chugging,
No one cared as he wasted away, rejected by his great railway.

In heavy coat, ragged and warm, in heat and cold constantly worn;
A stubbled chin, feet sandalled, bare, pepper and salt his chin
and hair.
Dreaming away each night and day above and near the old railway.

One day, in monsoon's heavy rain, climbing down his access drain,
He slipped and fell upon the rails; train driver tries to stop but
fails,
Ending a life so long, so grey, prisoner of Kenya's railway.

Brian L Heap

Grandma's Footsteps

Where did they go
  those tender feet
that splashed curled toes at the water's edge?
Where did they go
  those slender feet
that skimmed on tiptoe through the sun-warmed sand?
And where did they go
  those steadfast feet
that matched stride for stride, the pace across the dunes?
They're here, still here,
  the core in the fragile bones
that follow the searching stick in shuffling steps.

Jenny Johns

Stretching Out

I watch my mother growing older
A still intelligent, now confused, old lady
Hunting for her stick, her purse - and words.

Disempowered, she struggles
For that once-so-easy communication
Grasping the air, fearing pity.

I who am still articulate
Stretch out a hand to touch her arm, and smile.
One day I shall understand.

Helen Allison

Not Ready Yet

I shall not lie at peace within a gravelled grave
But toss and turn, until my white bones lie exposed
And I shall be again blown wildly by the wind,
Bathed by the rain in spring, whitened by winter snow.
        I am not ready yet to go.

Or I shall re-ignite my ashes to a flame,
St Elmo's fire will glow above the empty urn.
Touch the earth and you will find me burning still.
I shall not gently go to that eternal place.
        I am not ready, death to face.

Dorothy Will

Time

It is time to slow down
From the activity of my earlier way.
Time to *see* the beauty of God's world today;
Not in places far away
But, in the wild rose blowing
And hedges greenly growing,
Quite near to home,
No need to roam.
In such a world I may
Find time to be still and, in that stillness pray
For friends, to Him who made the world
And gave us friends, and gives us time;
Time to make ready, for that most wondrous world
Where other friends are met,
And where they wait our time.

Barbara Wedgewood

Growing Old

Youth has its sharp sweet sapling agonies
The ivied oak of age laments its anxious woes.
Outside the youthful herd, the lone ones pine, rejected.
More poignant in a crowd, the loneliness of the old.
A silenced voice has given quietus to the speaking minds
That once communicated with a smile or look;
And other voices merely speak with words
That are not heard with hearts.
The tale of days grows sweeter as they pass
Through every seasons natural joys, on ever swifter feet
Towards the time, when joys and sorrows past
The door swings open to that new friend, Death.

Grace Williams

The Lesson

Looking at her
my old schoolmistress
I suddenly realised
one day I'd be like her
  old
suddenly everything else
took on a strange perspective
my work, my family, my friends
they shrank into a fuzzy corner
one day I'll be like her
  old
and most things won't matter anymore
another voice was saying
revelations like this are too sudden
  actually
each wrinkle, white hair
takes time to set in
and yet another voice was saying
you've got forty-five years
to get used to it
but then I smiled, and saw
my once-young schoolmistress
wipe chalk words from the blackboard

Linda Marshall

Past all That

First the fear of dying
Then as old friends depart
Accept where they are lying
You can also venture

Pleasures remain despite
Arthritis, colitis and angina
Read the classics again
Revive the vinyl and potter
In the garden or try nine holes

Remember long legged girls and
Those mysterious parts one once knew
Put this aside and think of lunch
More accessible and maybe something cardinal
With a bustling riocca

The older one gets the easier
It becomes to enjoy because
The borrowed time syndrome pleases
One's sense of winning a game
And no one deprives you of a second martini
Because of the office or driving
You're past all that.

Stephen N Mackinnon

Senile Mother

Rather you were dead,
Than trapped, mindless,
In this maze
Of barren demeaning days.

Oh the fierce phoenix you were
In your silver-mercury years!
The rise of your smile,
The harvest in your heart,
And the diamonds among your tears!

Rather you were dust,
Than pawing, lost,
Through this cage
Of debris, festered by age.

Anne McAleavy

Unspoken Thoughts

You see - I do not want to die
For others' sakes, and not alone for mine.
Though others care - they care not more than I
For them - and though I pine
For friends and brothers who have gone,
I sorrow more for kinsmen left.
For all those leaving, rest is won,
But those the loved ones are bereft.
For when myself I take my leave
I have no comforter to send
To those I love and leave to grieve
And thus their sorrow mend.
It's not the leaving, more I fear
Bereaving those I hold most dear.

Victor Green

Requiem for Spring

Another Spring.
The sweet, soul-searching song of a thrush tugs at the heartstrings with an overwhelming desire.
For what?

Springs long gone.
When carefree youth strode loose-limbed
Through halcyon sunlit days.
Danced through woods awash with bluebell drifts.
Wandered by streams aglow with golden kingcups;
Or trod the thyme-scented turf on breezy moorland heights.

Age creeps on relentlessly.
The outward shell wrinkles and fades.
Limbs creak, joints ache, but the mind remains alert.
Music is sweeter.
Beauty is alive in little things.
Love makes no demands.
The woods wear a tender green.
Drifts of white blossom sprinkle the hedgerows,
Tiny balls of fluff scuttle around the surface of the stream.
Another Spring.
Too many gone. How many more?

Jess Chambers

Growing Old

The memory, divine receptacle
Of things taught or experienced
Linking childhood and sense of belonging
An ordered life, the tidiness of days

When the muddled mind falters
Remembrance drifts away
Facts, dates, faces, words take time to assemble
And the passing thought flees into oblivion

The ageing process bewilders
As communication becomes an effort
At first silly mistakes may amuse
But the verge of isolation beckons terrifyingly.

I Taylor

Disbelief

That can't be me in the mirror
That woman is far too old.
And yet she is wearing my shirt and jeans,
Is there something I haven't been told?

The grey-haired old hag with bifocals
On film, surrounded by youth,
I don't for a minute believe she is me
But I do know the people she's with.

That disturbing shop window reflection's
Of somebody else, never me.
I surely don't trudge with my parcels and bags
Quite so de-jec-ted-ly.

Only a year or two past
I was proud of the curves of my breast.
That fullness, with interest, has been re-located
Below what is left of my waist.

But there's no denying the camera.
Although I don't like it at all
On closer inspection I have to admit
It's probably me after all.

This picture is not what I wish
To present to the world round about.
It doesn't match up with the girl inside
Doing her nut to get out,

So . . .
I straighten my back, walk tall, tilt my head,
Put sparkle into my eyes;
Find the right muscles to draw up my mouth
And my image responds with a smile.

Maureen Harper

The Salesman

An old man, selling second-hand remarks
He held out, with a feeble hand, his book.
So different from those penitential sharks.
I almost (out of kindness) spared a look
But for his empty comment off the shelf
Prepared for busy ladies like myself.

'A woman's work is never done,' he said.
No pressure. He had nothing else to say.
'That's why she can't have any fun,' I said
Dryly, to no-one, when he'd gone away.

This quiet salesman tempted me to buy
His wisdom with a sympathetic eye,
A wisdom born out of a distant age
And paid for with an unfamiliar wage.

Heather Wastie

A New Visitor to the Home

'Why do you sit and gaze into space?'
'I am of no use to the human race.'

'There are things you could make'
'Stiff fingers ache.'

'A walk should do good.'
'My legs are like wood.'

'Books nourish the mind.'
'Not with eyes semi-blind.'

'There is food to savour.'
'But I've lost its flavour.'

"Music could cheer.'
'If my hearing were clear.'

'Should I go or stay?'
'Come some other day.'

Now that, at last, I am left alone
I'll go back to dreaming on and on -
Remember the dive through the curling wave
And Mendelssohn's music in Fingal's sea cave.
I'll compose a love letter in my own secret lair
Then walk on the moor with the wind in my hair.
Recall painting the shore from the islet strand,
Tasting salt on my lips as I row back to land.
Sense lithe fingers gripping on a tricky rock face
Till we stand on the summit and *marvel* at space.

Ruth Wallace

Only Half Their Age

Music thumps and young limbs
Jump and jerk like frenzied puppets.
Mandy's hair flies, wild and shining
As Billy leaps and shouts
With all the untamed energy of the young.

'Come on Granddad,' Mandy cries,
A small warm hand is felt in mine,
Two clear brown eyes in a grinning face
As I'm pulled protesting from my chair
To stamp and twitch and bend my aching knees.

Ah yes there was a time when
I had no need for glasses.
No need for putting things inside my ears
To help my hearing.
And rising from a chair was no big deal.

Sometimes I gaze across the yard,
The sunshine warm upon my balding head,
And everything is soft, diffused contentment.
The birds chirp loud, the cat's asleep,
And Ben, the dog, snores gently at my feet.

But other times the whole of me rebels;
These shaking hands, these watery eyes,
The wrinkled dried-up skin and sagging paunch,
The back that aches, the knees that creak
While inside, my mind is only half their age.

Pamm Morris

Winds of Life

Blow morning wind from the dawning east,
fresh and dew laden, sweeping away
the shades of night, the cloud of doubt,
the web of dreams, and let the hopeful ray
of new day bring enlightenment to the problems of reality.

Blow midday wind from the distant north,
icy sharp, letting your keen tang breathe
cool reason into the troubled heart,
soothing hot passions and hatreds, turning them
to zestful energy for the fulfilment of hopes.

Blow noontide wind from the sun-washed south,
warm and gentle, sweetly scented, giving
balmy airs to ease the weary limbs that have laboured
to achieve that of which they cannot know the right or wrong,
but only knew they worked for it in good faith.

Blow evening wind from the sunset west,
bringing the breath of dear loved moorlands,
tinting the sky with softly blended shades of memory
and I will know, when my work is done, that tomorrow
will dawn once more though I may not wake to see it.

For as I would be born to the east wind,
work with the north wind, rest under the south wind,
so 'tis in the west wind that I would die
and let tomorrow's winds make what they will
of my life's effort. Only let them bear in mind
that I did, even as they will believe they do,
the best I could, within the limits of my vision.

Jean Collins

Architect's Report

My insides are falling out
My cedilla façade is caving in
Though my thatch is sound enough
Passably maintained so far
My foundations much reduced
Have the strength of a blancmange
All in all the property
Worth about a peppercorn.
So, it's nearly time to die;
But, before the lease expires,
Maybe I could qualify
As an Ancient Monument.

Olga Townend

Here is the Work

From mottled mantelpiece wax rises tall to lit wick;
Flame strives high into airy rafters,
And in this light the old man writes,
Ink settling neat into lines scored deep into weighty paper.

Here is the work: the rising
falling patterns on the page.
From here the too-content are barred,
falsifiers tarred with black-letter truths.
Welcome here the shape-changing soot,
soft-flaking musty walls;
And here the flat proofs of truth
sparely transporting age to youth.

David Orman

Every Ten Years

The crown of the young man's head stares at her -
A double crown, twin whorls like eyes.
She returns to the task, completing the form,
Working her way down, squeezing letters into narrow boxes.
Now her own image stares at her from the passport page,
Brown curls, serious pale face,
Thirty-nine becomes forty-nine, the years slip by.
Colour of eyes: blue, colour of hair . . .
Her pen hesitates, she looks around for a mirror.
Her glance returns to the double crown,
'What colour would you say my hair is?'
'Grey' he replies, without looking up.
G-r-e-y fits in the boxes, her hand trembles,
Her face flushes hot as tears hit the back of her eyes.
He looks up and smiles, a cheerful grin,
'Cheer up, luv, you'll soon be on yer 'olidays.'
He bends his head to check the form,
The whorls return her gaze candidly,
Youth assesses age heedlessly.

Margaret Morley

With Age

The fires of passion dwindle, ash
of comfort settles in. Relentless years
whittle spoiling flesh and hurting power

is tempered. Content unravels knotted limbs;
in long small hours your breathing reassures,
like flickering lids on a waxen child.

There are no requirements to hear or say
'I love you.' Tomorrow if we wake
we must be alive, mustn't we?

Elizabeth J Hargreaves

Old - but Snappy!

Once, I walked lightly,
With limbs that, if
Competed with, could have
Sent a gazelle packing.

But now, my bones
Have started making sounds
That Red Indians
Try not to make
When they're tracking.

Betty Skipper

Too Kind

I had a fall.
A mis-step on a muddy kerb,
My bag and books followed me
To the pavement.
'Oh you poor thing.'
They grasped my arms
To haul me to my feet.
'Thank you. I'm quite alright.'
'You've had a fright.'
They held my arms quite tight.
'Please let me go.
I am alright.'
'My love, you must sit down.
Here is a chair.'
('I'm not your love!')
I want to swear.
Only my pride
Has had a tiny dent.
'Leave me alone. I'm all right!'
I wrench free and grab my things.
Why should I be polite?
'I really am alright.'
They're shocked. They stare.
They have been taught to care
For OAPs and animals.
'Too kind,' I snap
And save myself in flight.

Margaret Williams

Homing

'You're doing well,' I shout
into her better ear,
the soup I offer spoon by spoon
trickles down her chin
                                        she smiles
'Not bad for ninety years?' paper skin
crinkles round her eyes, her cheeks
a tracery of violet veins.

'I'll do it for myself,' she says
her hand unsteady on photograph
of smiling child
                              not now
but long ago
'I remember,' she recalls, 'the frock I wore'
but forgets the stove she lit an hour before.

The slow approach of Autumn damps the air
and strips the trees of faded leaves
that slip their hold
                                  descend
to drift in aimless circles
on a knife-edge wind
clouds obscure a waning moon.

Age comes upon us with the stealth
of Winter's shortening days;
faculties decline, leave shadows
of our former ways; a spent balloon hangs
limp on slender string
                                        waiting
to be free.

Jean Froggett

Tree Cycles

A chance meeting in the weary autumn park
after a year fragmented by futility and hard love,
proves unendurable in his supple face of lithe sustenance
and yet any chemical change is irrelevant.
He remains untouched,
in blissful ignorance under those giant loping trees,
eyes alive but full of youth's broken cliché
while my maturing disease
revels in the bleakness of every aching October sky.
Fear for his fresh complexioned mind percolates all sinuous channels
of tree and body,
as I become the oak: leaves lost and dead but a means of new life.
His coniferous shape remains:
intact and eternal but never provoking growth in his years.
What remains is a rich dilemma;
pulling him forward to sharp decay
or submitting me back to earthy blindness.

Iain McDaniel

Untitled

Dear God, I am not gentle!
Dear God, I am not kind!
Although I'm almost eighty,
Although I'm almost blind,
I swear to wage perpetual fight
Against the loving care
That's put me in an Old Folks' Home
And tries to keep me there.

Gwynneth der Parthog

Futures

Look at them, chair-bound,
islanded behind fixed trays.
They smile at shadows cast
by their dim memories upon senility,
and clutch the rugs upon their knees
feeling the texture of day.
They know the world is full of strangers.

Watching these decaying roots
the branches shake, silent
in the still day-room.

Pamela Sinclair

Never a Grandmother

I can tolerate
    the brag books,

admire
    the happen-to-be-here photos,

appreciate
    the proud achievements
    of all the clever darlings

but today
    I am undone
    by six short words:

    'Can I dance for you Gran?'

I laugh
    with my cherished, lucky friend
    at the improvised performance
    of her elfin granddaughter

but deep inside
    my aching womb
    is weeping the tears
    I cannot
    must not
    show.

Greeba Brydges-Jones

The Waiting

Around the walls they sit,
Eyes glazed or half closed,
Or fixed on the metallic picture-box
Like moths drawn to the light -
Waiting; waiting.

Not for them, the choice of time
Nor the manner of going.
Not for them, the choice of company
While they wait, some blissfully unaware,
Some painfully aware of their state.

Not for me, please God, to wait
In such a place; in such a state.
Not for me, to be but a duty to strangers.
Not for me, the indignity of not knowing,
Nor if aware, the sadness of knowing.

Margaret McDougall

These Hands

It's difficult to imagine that once these hands were
The scrabbling, demanding hands of the babe.
Learning the basic arts of living.
Growing into the craftsman's.
Moulded, by time and patience to become the hands they have
become.

Look at these hands,
Still now, in death form.
Never more to know the plane and saw.
Never more to feel life in the wood,
To create as they once did.

They leave instead a legacy of beauty
Within the voice of the violin.
Something that when these hands are dust
We will still accept.

Brenda Barry

Time Passing

How can the weeks go so quickly, how can it be
So long since our first loving and belonging?
How is it possible time should have stolen
Such a large share already?
        Sometimes I am afraid
        To hear a clock strike.

Or I lie wakeful in the pulsating dark
Feeling the pliant smoothness of your limbs
Folded into mine and hold you as you sleep,
Desperate: even as we breathe
        The minutes pass. Finally
        They are going to separate us.

There are the pictures focused on my mind,
As when you come towards me through the garden,
Eagerness quickening your step, eyes laughing.
Then all I want is that time should stand still
        The way my heart does
        Capturing the moment.

Because the store of memories to share
Seems finite now, I garner all I can
To hoard and cherish; a wasted afternoon,
An angry word, no more legitimate
        Now each year left
        Seems shorter than the last one.

There are days when I catch my breath, finding
A holiday half over, or a grey hair,
Or frost has killed the dahlias: the illusion
Of permanent Summer vanished in a gasp.
        Time passes quickly
        When you are so happy.

Isla Elliott

Untitled

When time has etched his wrinkles on my soul
To match the cobweb network 'round my eye
Then I will know that I have drained my bowl
For death is life when life's a living lie.

A change of heart's unable to renew
The passion manifest in belt or glove
Or vivify the dust-encumbered view
Back down the limb-locked corridors of love.

Time's darkest depredations of the flesh
Oppose the strong and reasoning mind within
My will and his prevailing will enmesh
I lose. Surrender now! Bow down! Give in!

And then my fuse-blown body he'll enclave
And he will toss me in the laughing grave.

Peggy Leng

Survival

Nostalgia cries out
from cracked pavements
and the sounds of Itma
straight from His Master's Voice.

Before my time, you say,
safe, still,
in the complacency of youth,
but wait,
soon, you, too, will know the truth,
soon, so soon, you'll feel
the cries of what is past.

You'll wonder how so many memories last
and
how time goes so very fast.

Pat Rigg

The Choice

If she was asked to live life over again from choice,
A vehement No! would cascade from her heart and mind,
She did not want again the stabs of emotional pain,
That seared her soul and serrated her thoughts,
putting a tortuous life on this sphere once again.
Now it was time to take comfort in the numbness of age
Where memory is dimmed by corroded arteries,
She decided that happiness was now with the anaesthesia of
the old,
An excuse to idle the time and count her daily dosage.
Look and be thankful for modern inventions.
Eyes riveted on the moving images telling of other peoples
lives.
Dramas of the strangers from the magic electric box,
Not today the glamour for her fictional fantasy,
Other people to dance and sing and cry, not her world
It was the privilege of age to watch through the veil.

Grace Graham

Now That I am Seventy-Five

I have had a happy life -
More joy than grief;
More sun than shade;
Good health and a loving wife.
We loved on through war, parted and afar;
Then savoured each new peace-time day
After all the war torn years of strife,
We had a calm and easy love of life.
Though penniless at each month's end
We muddled through, a happy man and wife.

When young a gypsy said to me
That even in deep water I would not get wet.
And so it seemed for an eternity;
Then fate took a hand; my wife fell ill and died.
Though family and friends were at my side
To comfort and to give me pity,
The zest had gone, and I had lost my stride.

And soon I faced the taxing plagues of growing old -
My frame was creaking, my foot less sure -
And each new weakness seemed so far from cure -
Days were dark, and even summer days so cold.
But then, one day, I felt new hope arise,
And time so grey gave way to summer skies.
My aches grew less, and then I grew in strength,
'Til through the haze I saw appear at length
The suffused splendour of a dawning day
An Indian Summer on its golden way:

And the walking boots I discarded last year
Will not go to the jumble sale just yet.

Eric Oates

We are Mere Tenants in This Spinning World

We are mere tenants in this spinning world
On time-share lease in measured nights and days
Where nature's threads are woven and unfurled

The fabric of our lives splays out uncurled
And breath is stolen in ten thousand ways
We are mere tenants in this spinning world

At speed of light we're grown and then are hurled
In puppetry of errors acting plays
Where nature's threads are woven and unfurled

On multi-coloured cords we're tossed and twirled
And all that weft we weave can not erase
We are mere tenants in this spinning world

In swathes of skein rotating we are swirled
Our foetal form unfolds its blueprint phase
Where nature's threads are woven and unfurled

The moment of conception is lace pearled
Anticipating vibrancy's brief blaze
We are mere tenants in this spinning world
Where nature's threads are woven and unfurled

Angela Platt

Looking Ahead

I had thought
Looking upwards
That the girls at the back
With know-all expressions
And breasts
Knew it all.
Yet standing at the back
Myself
I knew they didn't.

Then, looking at them
Proudly pushing prams
I thought
They have arrived.
But, pacing with my baby
In the middle of the night
I knew they hadn't.

In middle age
They seemed so calm
So self-assured.
Yet, coping with the change
Myself
I knew they weren't.

Still ahead
Confident
Into old age they stride.
But perhaps after all
They aren't.

June Gerrish

Does Growing Old Improve With Age?

At fifty plus, the whole world knows
You've made the next decade;
Mammography and HRT
Appointments will be made.

Late afternoon, on ITV,
One advert clearly aims
At fifty-fives, who're still alive,
To play endowment games.

And catalogues sent through the post
For thermals and flat shoes
Tell postmen you're now really old,
You're mail-shot, target news.

Too old for Teacher Training course,
Too young for pension pass,
Too 'rich' to claim for benefit,
Too 'poor' to join a class.

Does growing old improve with age
And bring its own reward?
Will I, with pension book at last,
Be able to afford

To learn a language, if I choose,
And travel cheap by bus?
Or in my thermals and flat shoes
Will I no longer fuss?

Sheila Fermor Clarkson

The Time Barrier

It's the Time you see
Not that it's running out tap-wise
From a broken cistern
(And effective plumbers live in dreamland)
But it's very speed increases all the while
So that yesterday was only half an hour ago
Childhood; last Christmas
One waits to pass through the time-barrier
When Now is Eternity

Michael Owers

Barefooting

'I remember when you danced barefoot
Swirling, solitary in the middle of the room.
Thirty years ago you danced barefoot,
And we all watched, and wondered about you.'

Now you just look
And stick labels on me:
Neat dressed woman,
Middle aged hair.
Don't just glance
And think that you know me:
Conservative,
Conventional,
C of E.

You cannot feel
The childlike spirit.
You cannot see
My mind soar free.
You cannot hear
My own secret music,
Or know I still dance
Barefoot.

Valerie English

Old Age

When old age creeps upon one
And things are wearing out
When one requires a wig on
And the limbs are full of Gout

When one has wrinkles in the skin
And living becomes staid
When one has got a double chin
And needs a Hearing Aid

When teeth are false or in decay
And spectacles aid the sight
When one forgets throughout the day
And cannot sleep at night

When one is always heaving sighs
And is scarcely ever cheerful
Is heading for a quick demise
So listen to this earful

Be thankful if you've got good health
Are comfortable and respected
Enjoy good friends and so true wealth
No more can be expected.

Leslie Ratcliff

Sonnet on Old Age

When shoulders stoop and chins begin to sag,
And old bones ache and muscles will not stretch;
When feet are flat and steps begin to lag,
And all day long one feels a tired wretch;
When wrinkles creep across a furrowed face,
And hair grows thin and eyes are dim and pale;
When memory's cap wears out like fretted lace,
And all that's left of one begins to fail;
When skin goes hoary like some ancient bark,
And thoughts begin to turn in on oneself;
When we grow querulous, and fear the dark,
And say farewell to confidence and health.
Then all we hope for is to find some way
To rest until the ending of the day.

Brian Gee

Will was Right

I reckon old Will was right
When he wrote that bit in Hamlet.
You know, about Sans everything.
Well, all right then, in 'As you like it'.

Yes, I know he wrote some others,
Besides a play called Hamlet.
All I'm saying is Will was right,
Sans everything just about says it.

Growing old might be all right
if your body worked well enough,
and you could get out and pull the chicks
and really do your stuff!

Growing old might be all right
on a good and steady income,
With an open sports and a natty cap
and a face that looked a bit winsome.

But when all you've got is a walking stick,
you'll find that this is true, mate.
Once you get to my age
there ain't much sport for you, mate.

All right, it's true I have a pint
and enjoy a pinch of snuff.
But I still wish I could pull the chicks
and really do my stuff.

I reckon old Will was right!
Where did you say you find it?
That's how your memory goes,
However much you mind it.

L Brewer

In the Event of my Death Abroad

If by chance, in some foreign field, I should die,
Bring me home in your mind, not in a box.
Leave there the tattered corpse, the tired heart.
Hold on to our love but leave the husk behind.

Place my ashes, in monumental urn,
Between the exotic bottles high in Nicky's bar,
Mummified in garlic, and the bouquet
Of harsh red wine, swathed in blue gaulois.

Or scatter them on the sun-dappled sand
Where the pines thin towards the sea, and the
Beach stretches white and low to each horizon,
Scoured by the cold Atlantic rollers

Entrust them to some rough but reverent
Fishermen, to cast in their creaming wake,
That my mortal parts can return to feed
The creatures that made my name, fed us all.

When you, sad, return, mourn me as I was,
In my prime. Feel my love when it had vigour.
We, faithless, require no carved marble,
No closed vault, to wait the final *Trompe*,
In your sweet heart and those we made together,
I'll live on.

Gerald Watkin

The Resolution

I'm pulling the plug on my life-support machine
by giving up my dream. It is the duty
of grandmothers to present the secure image -
the homely one of cardigans, coal fires and scones.
I'll suck peppermints instead of knocking back
the gin, buy 'Saga' now instead of reading 'She',
learn to love Catherine Cookson, let the dust
collect on 'Medieval History' and 'Heaven's Command'.
I'll fill my eyes with modern heroes on the box,
no longer pace the ramparts with La Vallette
or shout 'The Persians are coming' to brave Leonidas.
I will learn to knit and keep a button box,
differentiate between the daffodil and tulip bulbs,
bore my descendants with tales of 'When I was young . . . '
I'll acknowledge the arthritis in my knee,
the creak of aching joints; suppress the memory
of the tremors caused by your teasing hands.
My face will wear a tolerant fixed smile
and the screams will be contained inside my head.
My future will be safe and calm - reliable -
no problem to my children. They will not know
that I am clinically dead, that today,
with resolution, I pulled the plug on my dream.

The Ice Age of my heart moves inexorably closer in.

Jean Shaw

Ballad of a Grateful Woman

When I am old
I can be happy at last,
I will not care about my looks,
my body or the colour of my hair;
these middle years descending on me now
bear promises of that.

I spent
all the uncertain hours of youth
moulding nature's gifts, and errors,
into the contours of men's fantasies
so that they, insatiable, insensitive,
could dream their dreams;

virgin, wanton, earth mother
such were the seasons of my life,
and as the fleeing years
released me from each role
harder still the struggle when I strove
to paint upon the canvas of his desire
the ageless temptress;
half starved, powdered, painted,
offering myself up to his ageing, jaded palette
whilst he
sought youth in far more likely places.

I have worked hard for this,
for these grey hairs,
this passionless state, these moments of bliss,
and when age finally knocks upon my door
I shall open it with joy
and greet him as an old friend.

Ann Redcliff

A Rueful Rhyme

When the Grandchildren are grown I hope they will say:
'Oh Good! - Granny's driving over, in her Aston Martin,
to see us today.'
Far more likely it is, I fear, they will say:
'When will Granny die, so that we can drive her
Aston Martin away?'

Anne L Haines

Alas for Old Age!

Now colours are fun
When all's said and done.
(Yet some I avoid like the plague!)
So I choose with good care
The colours I wear,
And *pink* is reserved for *old age*!

I've tried all the greens
And some in-betweens,
Like pea-green, sea-green and sage.
They look good on girls
With triple-row pearls.
Which still leaves me *pink* for *old age.*

Just pity my plight
If forced to wear white!
I know I look languid and vague.
But let me tell you
I look good in blue.
I'll hate it in *pink* for *old age*!

With the passing of years
I'll revise my ideas,
Why - pastels may be all the rage!
Those soft, subtle tones
Go well with old bones -
And so does the *pink* for *old age*!

Some shades I've forgotten
And some are so rotten,
I haven't the nerve to presage.
Sufficient to say
I've worn most in my day.
Hey! Dig out the *pink* for *old age*!

Iris Allingham

Loneliness

Christ of my loneliness,
Christ bless my loneliness,
Christ be the guest
At the meal set for one;
Christ in the deaths so mourned,
Christ in the gestures scorned,
Christ by the friendships meant -
Never begun.

Christ in the silent day,
Christ in the silent night,
Christ be the letter
That never arrives;
Christ see my loneliness,
Comfort my loneliness,
Link to my loneliness
All lonely lives.

Christ take my loneliness,
Christ love my loneliness,
Christ who has called me
To stand apart;
Christ in my loneliness,
Christ be my loneliness,
Yours be the voice
That I hear in my heart.

Stephanie Batstone

Rôle Play

Birthday cards reveal the rôles,
Grandmother, mother, wife and sister, daughter, aunt -
No woman is an island unto herself -
But oh, for an island, on occasions
When you hear the chant
Of oh so many voices.

Small wonder that retirement means relearning
The joy of time completely spent on self.
Magic carpets of words and wealth
Of paintings.
Rainbows of paints and pastels that can recreate
The natural world so loved.
The balm and pain of music.

Joy, yes, and self absorption, true,
And a kind of satisfaction too.
No real fulfilment though.
I've lost the warmth of people.
I've lost the play -
Somewhere along the way.

Judy Barrett

Why go for the Gold

Life races by
Breaking each years previous record
Like an Olympian.
Naive not to assume the pace
Will be even quicker this year.
Life, flying by;
At undreamed of speeds -
To the finish line.

Trish Kelly

Diagnosis - MS

I stood alone at evening on the farm
To contemplate my life, now on the wane:
No longer can I boast a strong right arm,
I cannot now go striding down the lane.

The energy of youth begins to flag,
Time takes its toll with every passing day;
The feet that climbed so nimbly up the crag
Now stumble on a pebble on the way.

Before me lies the shadow of a 'Home',
Life stretches in a deep, descending path;
No longer can I dig rain-fragrant loam,
Or even climb unaided form the bath.

But in my eye there's still an eager gleam,
My body, not my heart's run out of steam.

Barbara Murray

Growing Old

My Child:
You ask what I have learnt from life
- Our greatest Mentor ever -
That I should now so sanguine be
With beliefs I cannot sever.

'Tis this:
In this ever changing world
'Tis good to strive for harmony,
Thus I accept folk as they are
And not as I wish them to be.

Gladys Dixon

Growing Old Gracefully

I worry about growing old.
I worry about whether I'll cope;
You see, I want to do it gracefully.
I want to grow old gracefully
bit by bit
Adapting to this change
and that
philosophically or pragmatically,
whichever is possible.
But, not a hope;
Not a hope in hell
That I'll do it
Never mind do it well,
For I'm just
Not
that kind of person.

Lynda Forbes Jones

Internal

It's many
a day
since I
performed a
'knees up'
of any kind
even investigative!
still
I remember
the drill so -
skip the spiel
and steady
with that
cold steel . . .
Dammit!
I wince
and wonder
why the thing
can't be padded,
and comfortable,
and less at
variance with
God's contrivance.

Elisabeth Spooner

An Age Old Poem

Why, when I am introduced to someone new
the first question asked is 'How old are you?'
Young or old, they all adore
to find out exactly what is my score
Does it matter the number of years
Surely only how one appears
So next time I am asked 'What is my age?'
My answer will be simply, 'I am at the elementary stage!'

Michele Wolf

There is a Hair Growing Out of my Chin

The chiropodist looks at my feet
The doctor looks at my notes
The home-help looks at my dust

No one looks at the hair growing
Out of my chin.

The postman sees my bills
The window cleaner sees my bed
The milkman sees I'm alright

No one sees the hair growing
Out of my chin.

My neighbour cares for my garden
My nephew cares for himself

No one cares about the hair growing
Out of my chin.

Pam Finch

Who Cares?

If the Minister of Health had to suffer for a day
 The indignities my Mother did (before she passed away),
She would realise how empty are the claims and promises
 That issue smugly from her mouth about the 'NHS'.

If the Minister of Health had a blindfold round her eyes,
 And her legs were tied together so she couldn't even rise,
And they sat her in the 'Day Room' where she had no wish to stay -
 She would call out to the nurses, but they'd look the other way.

If the Minister of Health were vainly calling from her ward
 She'd feel a deep distress at being utterly ignored;
She'd feel a desperate loneliness, a longing for release,
 From Hospital? From Life itself? A wish for simple Peace.

If the Minister of Health were left alone and had a fall
 She'd cry and moan and clench her teeth and then she'd
 grimly crawl;
At six o'clock one morning, on the floor, and feeling dead
 A nurse would come across her and drag her back to bed.

If the Minister of Health became bewildered, unaware,
 Bleeding, bruised and frightened - would The System really care?

J Machin

Looking Down

Red eyes, dabbed.
Abrupt family hugs.
The accomplished hearse.

And now, above the unfilled grave,
the fitted grass,
two late arrivals.

Plain wood.
Dribs of earth speckling her name.
A slant, single rose.

'No sun today. Sad for this'
says the old woman,
the woman on a stick.

'They should give money; flowers die'
- to the old man,
the man on a stick,

a white stick.

Geoffrey Holloway

Growing Old

What ages a man, for what earthen reason,
Can he be measured, like nature's three seasons
His essence of being, created and nurtured,
In Spring and in Summer, then falls, in the winter?

Did we praise our fine youth, in his comely new growth,
Making plans for tomorrow, not questioning truth,
Or the joy, as we tested and gained in our skills,
Maturing in health and the spirits' free-will?

Have memories become like a timely reminder
With patterns benign, in some woven behaviour,
For easing the problems of making decisions,
Nostalgic in thought, now replacing delusion?

Did we notice the change in the glass's mirage
As the coarseness and furrow, masked cruel the visage?
As paled the slack skin, and posture's tired slouch,
No avoiding this fading, it's winter's reproach.

Why the shadowy hope and vagueness in style,
Anxiety casts, a brief, plaintive smile,
With mincing of footsteps, now close to the wall,
Hides fears ever present, of ultimate fall.

It's not taken long to depress and convey
This framework of body, to pain and decay,
Where's the colour and perfume, of childhood in flower
Has winter descended and ticks our last hour?

P Homer

Tortoise Club

They got on at the bus stop,
took the stairs at a run.
How many of them were there?
Ten - their day had just begun.

Knapsack slung off shoulders,
boots clattering, all could be seen,
everybody chattering
as windows were wiped clean.

The fun and laughter of them
was infectious as they spoke,
on subjects from walks, muggings,
and overseas long-lost folk.

Who were they? Did you know them?
Kids on holiday from school?
No, the local *Tortoise Club*
who go rambling as a rule . . .

Thora Beddard

Autumn

If only we could die
As each year dies
With the sweet serenity
Of Autumn.

Not for us mortals
The September prelude,
When white mist
Fills the valley,
Jewelled cobwebs
Hang on brambled hedges,
And tall trees stand
In silent melancholy,
Ankle-deep in dew,
Their leaves limp
From a surfeit of green.

Nor the splendid adagio
Of October,
When calm lakes
Reflect the glory of the earth
As golden light
Sweeps the fells,
Floods the beechwoods,
And green becomes gold,
Or russet-brown;
When leaves curl
And fall, sun-dried,
In dusty heaps
For late winds to disperse
Before the long winter sleep.

But when we come to die,
There is only pain
And disillusion,
Unless we have found

Within ourselves
The beauty and permanence
Of the Spirit.
Then we may hope to die
Serenely
As each year dies.

Peter K Broadbent

Growing Old

God 'a mercy
Give me a word or words
To stir my failing heart
In praise again
Of sights and sounds
I've so long seen and heard.

My sad unsteadied steps
To firmness, and exultant
Joy suffuse my breast
As once it did.

I'm old. Give me the stars
To move my chest in sobs
Of joy, as once it did.

Ah! Hapless thought,
Go I must to rest, they say.
Not best. Inevitable
As those same stars
And these same steps.

S H B

The Warning

We all have our problems, I think you'll agree,
But mine are more than most, or so it seems to me.
I'm a slave to the sink, to the pots and the spuds,
I know what 'cuts grease' and the best 'bubbly suds'.
I've just done the washing. It's out on the line,
There's threatening cloud, but I hope it keeps fine.
And now if I'm lucky, I'll have a short break,
On with the kettle and some tea I'll make.
I mustn't forget, I've the veg to prepare,
No rest for the wicked. It doesn't seem fair.
There's the silver to clean and the brasses as well.
I've just broken a plate, and there'll be merry hell
When the wife comes back home. She's just gone out shopping.
I'd better get on. The floor really needs mopping.
Sometimes I wish, for miles I could run,
Because it's true to say, my works never done.
So listen you fellows when retirement draws near go find
a hobby to do,
I'm afraid if you don't, the wife surely will it's into the
kitchen for you.

C L Shurie

The Impossible Dream

No thank you God, though you offer fresh eyes,
a magnificent gift, and so kind.
Just to see the colours of nature once more?
Well, I've managed so far . . . though I'm blind.

Good health? . . . no thanks, albeit wracked with pain,
and cannot remember the last time I ran.
It would be nice I suppose to get up and dance,
but on reflection, I'll stay as I am.

Money you say? . . . as much as I want?
to open each and every door?
In my youth that's just what I craved for,
but now I think I'll stay poor.

But wait! dear Lord . . . there *is* one thing,
one gift I know that I lack.
If you want to give me a treasure beyond compare,
then just once . . . let me put the clock back!

D P Glanville

Stars Must Know

At last my hour has come
A night full of expectation
Many thoughts fill my head
Now the hoped for realisation.
I skirt the streets of shame
Stand alone in a crowded bar
Dance with my faceless friends
I've never known who they are.

Flames of resistance burn brightly
I move in a silent desperation
Time and tide stalk like hunters
Blow coldest winds of alienation.
Empty streets in the midnight hour
Confront me with a futile existence
Prostitutes drift like silent spectres
I harden my heart to persistence.

Where lies one crack in the clouds
A chance of friendship, conversation?
I find clubs, drink several beers
Girls pose in a mocking temptation.
A night ends with terrible sadness
I mourn the death of another day
Hours turn into weeks, later years
Stars know people must live this way.

John Farrell

Westerns

Along the cinder track between old houses
Comes the no-hoper,
Leaning on a stick, head down
Into the wind.
Shabby shoes scuffle through dry leaves
As he follows his Friday path
To the corner shop.
Pulp westerns come in today,
'Winchester Westerns for Excitement'
Say the gaudy covers,
And he permits himself
A slight lightening of spirit.
In summer he reads them on a bench
Outside the fish shop,
In winter in his cold back room.
This tired old man,
Living a grey life,
Has a secret self, golden and strong,
That rides the range forever.

Judy Diss

Geriatric Ward Chesterton Hospital Cambridge

They are not for me,
Those poet's thoughts of immortality.
The years press heavy
And sleep is hard to find.
My soul is free,
Though body has paid life's levy;
All action now revolves within my mind.

The mist of time is all I see,
Projected there, my memory.
Youth's Spring flies quickly
And soon the colours fade.
You just see me,
I look so old, so sickly,
But within my brain remains the life I made.

Once I had my privacy,
And faced your world with dignity,
Before the years ensnared.
Within time's endless cage,
What will be - will be,
But I am still quite unprepared,
And find no recompense, in age.

Brian D Thompson

How Did I Come to This?

How much longer can this last
will someone take me now
if I had thought I'd come to this
I would have ended it somehow

I look at friends - some better off
some others just like me
engaged in a survival war
against society

Oh I've had money - in my day
I earned hand over fist
growing old and needing others
just wasn't on *my* list

The two of us were having fun
the best of friends we were
oh yes there were vague thoughts of life,
the universe - but rare

She's gone now - and I never dreamed
how life could drain away.
Not only hers but mine as well
I hate each passing day

But wait - she's gone a long long time
am I confused again
the fear of going outside my door
tears pieces from my brain

The rhythm of my life has changed
The neighbours say I am deranged
I cringe at their cruel jibes

I cannot clean this place so well
Oh *God!* it is a living hell
What's happened to my pride

John Gillespie

Mobility

Mobility, mobility, there's nothing like mobility,
To walk around, to run around, with unimpaired
agility.
I had this power when I was young, this
marvellous facility.
I took it all for granted then, as natural
ability.
But with the years my legs have lost a lot of
their virility.
The unrelenting march of time has lessened their
utility
Or as they say in USA, 'reduced their capability.'
I hope there'll be no worsening, but 'medical
stability'.
The trouble has not reached my mind or thoughtful
sensibility
And up to date I don't expect incipient senility.
In dreams some nights I walk again, but day
brings disability.
I try to face my present state with imperturbability
And with an inner sense of peace, and humour and
tranquillity,
Rejoicing that my mind is free, to range with *real*
mobility.

Norman Hurst

Untitled

Why, at such an early age,
Has life begun to fade
So quickly from my every limb -
Has death upon me preyed?

Earth was ne'er so bright and clean
As it now before me stands -
Now, whatever lies in my grasp
Seems precious to these hands.

Michael J Erian

Untitled

Good morning old Mr Pitts, you're eighty today,
The usual - tea, toast, eggs -
                                        and a moan?
You've employed me two winters and more,
Just this day could you smile, not a glare
                                        and a groan.

Snapshot of a child in a large country house,
Snapshot of a man in fine clothes
                                        and a car,
Third age brings no cheer you still crib
Tight lipped, bitter words, you've a sneer
                                        and a snarl.

Cynical, selfish, frosty fart,
Hopeless, hapless, withered wart.

Hello young Catherine you're eighty today
Let's celebrate with iced bubbly wine
                                        and a cake.
We've been best mates for summers galore
Though you're older than me by years
                                        and a week.

Childhood; no father, no money, much want
Adulthood; hard work paid for play
                                        and a hat,
Third age brings no wealth you won't harp,
Flushed faces, soft voices share a laugh
                                        and a chat.

Solid, selfless, frothy fun
Honest, helpful warm hearted one.

Margaret Harvey

Sea Gardens

We are latecomers to these sea gardens,
Walking in mist,
Behaving as if we were young,
-In these sea gardens -
Late birds, in winter mist.

We have not exactly spring to our step;
On the cliff walk
Slow our ways: climbing, descending,
- Grey goats you might say -
Conversing, as we walk.

We have fond regard for these wind-bent trees,
Leaning as we . . .
Weathered, by the parallel years,
- Old friends we love most -
Bent trees, alive as we . . .

Our coats are somewhat damp from the sea air,
Salt-tanged our breath,
Late Chrysanths' we lay claim to be,
- December yet flowers -
Showing our winter breath.

We can foresee Spring on these zigzag paths,
These cliff-gardens
Where, tenacious . . . we cling on
- Sere leaves in chill fog -
Late to these sea gardens.

Peter R Dennis

Mirror Image

That guy in the mirror is much older than me
He's well down the road to senility.
Masses of wrinkles and too much grey hair
Worn out and haggard, not the least debonair.

A bottle man maybe, too many late nights
Drifting perilously close to his last rites.
Yet - yet - that nose is familiar and the stained yellow teeth
Propped up by two chins with flab underneath.

No - no - it's definitely not me
I'm just not that short
And he's facing starboard
While I'm facing port!

Thank God!

Mike Devereux

Thirty Thousand Nights

My locked, Jack frosted, cold cracked limbs
Melt with the melting night,
The sunless time
First welcomed, held me photographed,
My heavy body snapped
Too sapped, to break its aged timeless fight.

The bird-brought dawn that culls the cold from flesh
Scours the darkened room,
And fills my past cold pumping heart
To start, afresh
The burning, gushing, blood rush dance, that is my body's jest.

So my warming, sun dusted skin, flowers in the blooming light,
Can it defy another of these thirty thousand deaths?
These thirty thousand nights?

John M Rimmer

It Happens to the Best of us

I wonder why so many dread
The time that's called 'old age'.
We often hear the young ones say
'Don't let me reach that stage.'

But those we see with walking-sticks,
And hair that's turned to grey,
Were once the boys and pretty girls
Who danced the night away.

They can't go roller-skating now,
So take the dog for strolls,
And many find their happiness
In fishing, books or bowls.

Some people, in the best of health,
Seem old at forty-five,
While others reach the age of ninety,
Glad to be alive.

These grans and grandpas have a place
In families everywhere.
Their years of vast experience
Are what we need to share.

If people moan because they're old,
And aches become a curse,
They should be glad for what they've got;
The alternative is worse.

This life is what we make of it,
We only get one chance.
The last sweet waltz of eventide
Should be the greatest dance.

Sybil Hurcomb

Nursing Home

The world from my wheelchair is so very small
My bedroom, the lounge, and connecting hall,
Each day I travel this very short route
To sit with the feeble, the deaf, and the mute.
The room is full of assorted old dears
Who dribble, and shout, and cry out their fears.
Oh I'm cared for and fed, and they're ever so kind
But they talk to me as if I hadn't a mind.
The indignities you suffer - I try not to care,
But to come to this Lord, it just isn't fair.
I had a nice little home and a dear little cat
Then I had a fall - and that was that.
It's the privacy I miss that I had before, and the
peace and quiet behind my own front door.
I do have lots of visits from family and friends
They bring the latest news and the current trends
They cheer me up, and then they too depart
But they leave a warm glow right deep in my heart.
O Lord, why do we olduns continue to live,
I suppose it's because we still have something to give,
But at my age I can't think what it can be
'Cos tomorrow my friends I'm one hundred and three!

Pauline Harley

On Growing Old

How funny I was! - but I was harrowed,
Hollow in tummy and pale of face.
How levelled my pride! - Though I had triumphed,
Keeping my placing in the race.
How memory takes essential samples,
Clearing the issues in after years.
How jolly is Age now understanding,
Laughing at all the youthful tears!

Memory weak? But judgement wise.
Getting stiff? Then exercise.
Reading dim? Then roll your eyes.

Counter every daily strain
By bending muscles back again,
Proper balance to regain.

When you feel your sun has set,
Square your shoulders, up you get,
Believe me, you're not finished yet!

Betty Murray

Stillborn

Contorted he falls
A broken old man
Writhing to crumble
Yet motionless still sleeping
To be a child once more
Plead worn out faded eyes
Gaunt hunchbacked trees
Convulsively outstretched
Search for mournful praise
Silently they have breathed
A fossilised impression
No more . . .
Waiting while the hours fade
Keep young now life can only be
That which you have seen
Old before the first scream
An embryo in silence
Unborn and cold
Motionless still sleeping
Immortalised like stone
Old men who crack
Fall aching to the dust
That parts to greet these . . .
Tired faces with tired eyes
Pushing in our everything
Flies around the maggot meat
A rotting old man
Decomposing day from day
Stillborn
Yes we are.

Matthew Porter

The 'Plaint of the Unmarried Daughter

Whatever shall I do with Gran?
        She's nearly ninety-three!
The day her widowhood began,
(To terminate her 'Golden span')
The other members of the clan
Thought, as I hadn't got a man,
        She'd better live with *me*!
Whatever shall I do with Gran?
        Oh! Why must it be *me*?

Whatever shall I do with Gran?
        She's daily getting worse.
She isn't spick, she isn't span
Her sanitation's far from 'san'
She cannot use the salle-de-bain,
Although I do the best I can,
        Commoding makes me curse.
Whatever shall I do with Gran?
        She really needs a nurse.

Whatever shall I do with Gran?
        She can't get out of bed.
It's - Can I hear the bell? - I can!
Wipe up the drool that fell? - I can!
Endure the awful smell? - I can!
The faeces and - the *hell* I can!
        I'm going off my head.
Whatever shall I do with Gran?
        She's worn me to a thread.

I dread her death, though it will mean I'll
        End these weary days here.
I'll wipe out all the years between, I'll
Seek fresh fields and pastures green, I'll
Be the wife I might have been, I'll
Hope to die before *I'm* senile,
        Slowly going crazier.
Oh! Knowing what old age can mean, I'll
        Pray for euthanasia!

Miriam Greenwood

Old Age - a Celebration

My youngest friend is eighty six.
I'll tell you what she does for kicks.
In summer time she rides her horse
Over hills, through broom and gorse,
And sometimes calls on me to say
What fun she's had on Star today.

I went to lunch with her last week
And found her in a fit of pique.
Her hearing aid had broken down.
She'd driven twelve miles into town
To get it fixed, just to be told
That model was no longer sold.
So mending it could not be done.
She told me if she'd had a gun !

Back to the lunch - she'd cooked a trout -
Delicious, with the bones all out.
And though her teeth do not quite fit
She's taught herself how *not* to spit!

After lunch I saw her beds
Gay with flowers, pinks and reds.
Latin names tripped from her tongue,
Her memory is ever young.
Her energy I then admired
And asked her if she ever tired.
As she bent to pull a weed
Her answer sounded like a creed.
'If I allowed myself to flop,
Like a clock I think I'd stop.'

Ann Mather

Viewpoint in Sarajevo

The man next door who is seventy-five
cannot decide
whether to live now that freedom had died
cannot decide
now that his Nation is submerged by a tide
of hate and despair
poisoning the air
of Freedom . . .

cannot decide . . .
whether to ride out the tide of hate
cannot decide
whether it is worthwhile to wait
or maybe to join in the endless debate
armed with the thoughts of reason . . .

Geoffrey Parker-Platt

I'm Going to be a Granny!

I'm going to be a granny!
Now, that wasn't too painful was it?
(I've said it before, but behind a locked door)
And now I've come out of the closet.

OK there are worse things to be,
And I've tried to be terribly brave,
But I haven't reached forty - I want to be naughty
And grannies should always behave.

Well, I shan't be a regular granny,
I shall do all the things I should not,
I'll wear red suspenders, I might watch 'Eastenders'
And 'Dallas' and 'Neighbours' - the lot!

I'll listen to Bon Jovi records,
Wear mini skirts up to my bum,
I'll wear six-inch heels,
What I can, I'll reveal
Oh yes! What a tart I'll become!

Well OK, I'll come back down to earth,
It's a fact that I just have to face;
If the Gods do decree that a granny I be,
Might as well be a granny with grace.

I suppose I had better accept it,
It comes to us all in the end,
If I played the right card I could be avant garde
And grannies may yet be the trend.

Yes! I'm going to be a granny (and)
With superior tone I shall add;
'My dear it's the rage! - you're still not? - at your age!
I'm so sorry - how terribly sad!'

Jinny Owen

The Tourists

It was cooler in the meadow
By the softly flowing river,
Seeing in the summer distance
Cambridge with its misty towers.
We chose an inn with a flowered yard
And a tired old tree leant downwards
To the ground, graceful in submission.
It gave us shade to eat our lunch
Alone in ghostly quiet and
Springtime's sudden heat, where fat dogs
Lay panting by the shadowed wall,
And yes the clock said ten to three.
We smiled into each other's eyes
And toasted secret days when no
Cold corners cut across our lives.
A toast to love, well-worn perhaps
But constant, 'Like the clock,' he said.

Elizabeth Clifton

Untitled

I soar to the summit
on the wings of joy.
My spirit exults to be free
and alone in the pure, sparkling air
and yet -
The earth waits.

Down, down I plummet;
I am caught in the web,
Twisting and turning
In the strong, silken thread,
and still -
The earth waits.

The earth waits
with its powerful plea -
Break the links in the chain,
Be released from the pain.
Come, come to me.

But the bonds of love still bind me
and my spirit remembers the heights.
I'll take up the challenge of life again
with the promise of joy regained,
and now -
The earth must wait.

Kitty Bould

Mid Sixties Sonnet

Externally my mirror shows for me
Wrinkles, grey hair, the loss of youthful bloom.
But I've no time or tears, my heart's no room
For grieving for the flesh that used to be.
Admittedly the body will not work
As once it did. It tires, it aches, it's slow.
Internally vibrates life's same glad glow;
No pointless sad bemoaning wishings lurk.
Roses still smell as sweet, birds wing and sing,
Stars shine, sun smiles, seas sparkle to delight,
Pets comfort, love is warm and friends all bring
Joy in a world that can't be ever bright.
Youth's striving music's fitting for the young.
Age thankfully hears happy songs still sung.

Patricia Richardson

No Fool Like an Old Fool

Feeling cold
I hold my hands to a young fire
Beautiful and attractive.
It warms me
Then it blazes higher
Burning hotter.
I ought to move
But I have had a long day
And feel lethargic,
A little stupid with drink.
I remember other warmth,
Think I am old and tough
And can withstand the heat
Without being burned.
So there I sit
My face getting redder,
Shoes cracking,
Sweating like a pig
Until my eyebrows singe.

Move, you fool, move!
Soon you will be a mass of flame.

Ralph Stephenson

Alzheimer

At first she was merely forgetful,
But sank into rapid decline,
'Til all she remembered was childhood,
And spoke in a petulant whine.

She would not get up in the morning,
Denied she had wetted the bed,
Then sulked or went into a tantrum
When later she had to be fed.

Suspicious of capsules and tablets,
Convinced they would do her no good,
She thought her relations were jailors,
And sneaked from the house when she could.

Through violence and torpor he nursed her,
Her husband these sixty-two years,
But as she was dying she pierced him
With words that reduced him to tears.

'Who are you?' she shrieked in her frenzy,
'I've never seen you in my life!'
Heartbroken, he managed to mumble,
'I'm Jim, love, and you are my wife.'

Brian Mitchell

Reflections

At sixty-three
I have to pee
Each night at three
Oh to be
Just twenty-three
On bended knee
Or thirty-three
Top of the tree
Or forty-three
Drifting free
Or fifty-three
Little else to see
But no, I am sixty-three
Content with me.

John Clare

Untitled

The nurse spoke softly, gently
And told me you were dead
'He didn't suffer dear,
And now he is at peace'
Round and round in my head
Went your words,
My amulet of love
Throughout so many years,
'I will always love you
Until the day I die'
O, My dear,
How could you go before me?
I do not understand.
And will this pain
Which fills my heart today
Ever cease?

M P Ward

Peace

Give me the peace
Of a sunlit wood
Or the quiet of a family, grown
Let my thoughts spin, within
My mind - alone.
I do not wish
For another voice
To fill my time-torn days.
When my years are spent, and bent
My back, with age
I'll waste no tears
In vague lament
That loneliness shall cease.
In a room, soft lit I'll sit
Myself, at peace.

Edna Weaver

Old

Old is frisky
Old is fun
Old is having an elephant's bum.

Old is ridiculous
Old is a joke
We start out as tadpoles
Just to end on a croak.

Jane Cockerham

University of the Third Age

I wuz wundrin' now that I 'ad reached retirement,
What I could ever do to fill me time.
I'd gathered skills an' knowledge in six decades,
To go an' waste it all would be a crime.

One day when all seemed very bleak an' cheerless,
I sawra notice 'bout the 'U3 Age?'
It offered courses - could this be the answer?
I cast a jaundiced eye across the page.

An' then I saw one called Creative Writin',
'I knows you can create,' me 'usband sed.
'Jus' see if you can *write* sumthin' excitin',
An' I can get some peace in' stay in bed.'

So nervously I drove off to the meetin'
Where other 'opeful writers gathered round.
We 'eard what we'd be doin' in the classes,
'An' left with 'omework! 'Jus' like school,' I groaned.

We learns about the art of composition,
We reads our 'omework over to the group.
T'aint easy to be told it needs re-writin'.
Our teacher really puts us through the 'oop!

(Thass bad! I've used one of they cliches!)

So though it's very 'ard and needs much thinkin',
You'll find we all returns week after week.
An' if we're not great authors, it don't matter,
Companionship an' fun is wot we seek!

Cynthia Manning

Thank you for the Days

(A Day in the Movement of the Life-Clock)

A beautiful day
But the life-clock ticks.
This summer's day
Is a frame at the flicks,
A split second in a short movie.

With cigar and cup
Still the life-clock ticks
A stolen hour,
A sorry mix
Of possession and loss,
A grain of sand through the waist of the hour glass.

Carpe diem!
Yet the life-clock ticks apace,
'Til the alarm rings out
And all these days are one,
A wreath of marks around life's clock face.

David J Ayres

The Stick People

At noon each day they come,
Leaning on sticks or wheeled
To the eating place,
(View of the lake, the flowers,
If one can see,
Sound of the dove, the lark,
If one can hear.)
Here they feed, or are fed;
Taste, or do not;
Speak, or stay quiet;
If quiet, lost in the maze, perhaps
Of paths their nimble feet once trod,
From which they find no path
That leads to Now.

One man, reduced by palsy
Invented once a glass
That would not shatter,
This helps him now,
To pay for care
That will not shatter.
Another keeps her room,
Her last refuge from Death
Who, once outfaced
In Nazi days
Affects indifference,
Stays well away,
Content to wait;
And wait . . .

Not quite of their clan,
Crutches as yet my temporary support
I ask one: 'What's it like?
Are *you* inside
Those shaking hands,
Those knocky-knees

That only just support
Your giant frame.
The *you* that was *you*?'
The answer's in the eyes
The way it always was.
Eyes speak when tongues are tied
Or almost so, responding truth,
'I will be me until I cease to be.'

Mary Bourne Richmond

Fair, Fat and Fifty

I wish I'd looked after my skin
But the wrinkles have firmly set in

I wish I'd been active with swimming and sport
And strengthened my muscles until they were taut

I wish I'd gone running and not stayed in bed
I'm out of condition with middle aged spread

I wish I'd not eaten puddings and pies
And biscuits and chocolates and crispy french fries

So I've bitten the bullet and enrolled at the gym
I work out and weight lift and go for a swim
I ache in the back and the bum and the thigh
I'm panting and sweating . . . I think I'll just die

They measured my fat and checked my heart-rate
And then sat me down and gave it me straight
I'm very unfit, I must change my ways
I feel rather ill and my eyes start to glaze

But they show me no mercy, as I climb on the bike
Do five minutes cycling, or ten if you like
And then move on to the jogging machine
I have to confess I'm not really keen

My legs are like jelly, my heartbeat is racing
I have to keep running, it's supposed to be bracing
I've had more than enough, I'll just lie on the mat
'Come on Granny Smith, let's burn off some fat'

I'm finding it tough . . . I'm ashamed to admit
That I'm fifty and fat and very unfit

The good news is that in six months' time
I'll be healthy and lissom and right in my prime
Let's toast my new lifestyle with a glass of chilled wine
Next year I shall say that I'm just forty-nine!

Gillian Smith

Thoughts on Growing Old

Spring and Summer have long passed by,
But Autumn lingers on,
In a touching smile, still twinkling eye,
While Winter waits; not long.

'Til snowy fingers find, then touch
And brush your hair and brow,
To tell the world your youth has gone,
Old age steps forward now.

When shuffling gait and bending knee
Betray your secret dread,
How, sweet to dream still youthful dreams,
Fear not the path ahead.

For Winter can be beautiful,
Though days are bleak and cold,
There is a stillness and a peace
That comes with growing old.

The days that are gone to memory's care
Age cannot weary nor fade,
You will find a new Spring at the close of the year,
When the sunshine of youth turns to shade.

Jean P Bidmead

The Third Age

We joined U3A so to be in the swing,
And none of us now will be out on a limb.
With so many friends on a Thursday to greet,
A smile and a welcome whenever we meet.

We patiently wait in the school hall, until
Out of their classrooms the juveniles spill.
Tumbling and surging and chewing withall
To get to the playground to play with a ball.

We ease to our places in tiers, row by row;
Dissemble the news - conversation does grow!
Then order is called, the authoritative tone
Welcomes speaker and members, and all settle down.

The leaders of groups state the pleasures to find
By joining the ranks of the serious mind.
The music and French - don't forget the next walk,
Antiques, current-affairs which, of course, is all talk!

Pondering the poets is some people's choice,
And studying drama allows them a voice.
Then up stands the speaker to give us his say,
Projector is fiddled and coaxed into play.

Lights out, and a hush - is that a slight frown?
It is only the first slide put in upside down.
The speaker talks on, he not one wit abashed.
(The projector adjudges which picture is flashed!)

The lecture goes on to devouring ears.
The end of the morning assuredly nears.
A sincere vote of thanks, and the company clap,
Then we all amble off for some lunch - or a nap.

Lilian Mantle

Nowt

Ee I'm reet sorry, ivrybody sez,
to 'ear you're badly like, angina tew!
An' dew you hev mich pain? Think on an' dew
no more ner wat you must. Be'ave yersen.
Tek care nah. 'Ope you'll sooin be on t'mend.
It mun be gallin' fer a chap like you
'oo's allus bin so active like, an' 'oo
nah finnds 'is ewsfulness is at an end.

I nod mi 'ead, as if mi day wer past,
a brokken-dahn machine o' no more ewse;
but laffin' up mi sleeave wi' the thowt
'at my bone-idle nature finnds at last
a copper-bottomed watter-tight excuse
nubdy can argue wi' - for dewin' nowt!

Kenneth Wadsworth

The Last Laugh

Old Age comes stealthily
    Frightening the Child inside,
And with the breath of the Bogey in my hair
    Beckons me to ride.

Old Age is here so soon,
    But with a conspiratorial grin
He takes bites of my daily memory
    Making a joke of remembering.

Old Age creeps up as bones begin to creak
    Further and further moves the ground away.
So relax, - enjoy those meals in peace,
    For exercise is fading day by day.

Old Age laughs as my chassis rusts,
    Holes appear and a vital item falls,
Humour saves the day; - it is absurd
    To feel so virile yet the engine stalls.

Old Age smiles, - a nuisance, but not sad,
    Don't take him seriously, - see the funny side.
If you die laughing, - yours is the day!
    His is the pain, the fear, - but yours the pride!

Elizabeth Stanley

I'm Not Sad

I think old age can be quite sad
When I think of the things I haven't had.
The chance of travel in exotic climes,
Making love in woods of scented pines.
If Bob, or Dick, had truly cared,
I wonder how I would have fared.
But while I muse I don't regret
The lovers who I can't forget.

I think old age can be quite sad
When I think of the things that I have had.
A face once smooth now etched with lines
Is one of many telltale signs.
The eyes, now just not quite so bright
Herald years to come of fading sight.
But long known friends are just the same,
And we often talk of - 'Whatsisname'.

I think old age can be quite sad
When I think of the things that I have had.
A body slim and full of zest,
Now aches and pains force me to rest.
But though I sit with aching joints
There are so many saving points,
A phone call from excited Son
A Grandmama I've just become.
So I am really very glad,
Old age for me is not that sad.

Janet Bradley

November Men

Once again leaves are turning, falling,
Frosted, silvered, blazing yellow and brown;
In a red dawn of a November day
Old men are about their remembering
Of pals who will never grey as they;

Like November's leaves, wrinkled, sere,
Eyes often dimmed by a rheumy mist,
Limbs withered, bent as some old tree,
Of all things novel they have a fear
They are yesterday's men, 'tis easy to see;

November, a month that mirrors their ageing
A time of year that aches their bones,
Now they see mortality drawing nigh,
Not a vague disregarded darkening
That in their youth never caught their eye;

Some sit silent, in memory wrapped,
Others gather to talk of days long gone,
By group reminiscence evoke their youth
To savour it, as a prime vintage newly tapped
And with hindsight embellish plain truth;

November men, cling to past glory,
Calling past times 'Those good old days'
Boring young men with 'I remember when'
Trotting out some old hack of a story;
I know, I muster with those November Men:

Stan Dodd

Life's Tree

The tree of life is three score ten
As in youth, your just a sapling
When your leaves are seen, a glossy green
But before you know what's happening
Young as you are, the time's not far
When green leaves, turn to amber
High hopes just like the Autumn leaves
Turn pale in late September

Ambition's tree is in full bloom
When one is in his teens
No aches or pains, or cloudy gloom
Now you are full of beans
So gather rose-buds, while you may
For time in velvet shoes
Silently rubs out the years
And with them all our woes.

The troubles of our yester years
Are now forever gone
The ones that still, may bring the tears
To every one belong
So don't look to the future
Or either to the past
But tackle each day as it comes
And life will longer last

For so it is with man and maid
When beauties age is o'er
Our debt to nature, we have paid
And pass this way no more

John Redmond

Parable

Young Father Tom
Went down a bomb
At the Century Halls last night.

The clerical star
Of the steel guitar
Fair set the town alight.

To wild applause
He raised for the cause
Close on two thousand pounds

As the concrete walls
Of the Century Halls
Shook to his mighty sounds.

Three miles away
Old Father O'Shea
Knelt in contemplative prayer

In the semi-light
Of the late Summer night
At Saint Joseph's in Salisbury Square.

While his curate played
He felt afraid
And he thought it exceedingly odd

That such secular forces
Supplied the resources
To pay for the work of God.

Gerard Owen

Regrets

The cupboards are less crowded -
One dress for best occasions will suffice
With another waiting for a wedding
Or, sooner still, a grandchild's baptism,
But no need for much more.
Outings are less frequent now
Visitors are fewer
What's the use of hoarding?

The bookshelves are less heavy -
Some novels to be read again perhaps,
And tomes advising on the garden,
But most have been passed on
To local car-boot sales.
Just favourites grace once-sagging shelves,
Some hiding letters
For beloved grandchildren.

But the mind is crowded still, and heavy,
Sometimes with past regrets and memories
Kindness not returned before it was too late
Places not visited while stamina was high
Diaries not kept before the memory failed
Calls not made while travelling was a joy.

Ann Green

In my Third Age

In my third age, my terrible anger is this:
I have not been able to stop
Mankind's incredible cruelty to animals;
Deliberate, gauged, thought out
And carried out, cruelty.
Caged and beaten, starved, neglected,
Experimented upon.
Tortured, hunted, terrified -
Not for food but 'fun'.
'A laugh,' 'sport,'
'Good' people's pets in hutch and cage.
My terrible anger is wasted, in my third age.

I have not been able to stop
Mankind's unbelievable cruelty to animals.
Don't say I should care more about people,
Animals are also a sort of people,
And, besides, I *do* care about people.
But who shall speak for the dumb?
Who shall protect these other sort of people?
My terrible anger scorches me, in my third age.
The bears! Oh, the bears!
Have you seen the pictures?
Their bile can help ease cancerous man, they say.
But *why* should man be saved at such expense?

Mankind deserves exactly what it gets.
Exactly what it gets, so it deserves.
My terrible anger will not subside,
Will accompany me to the end of my third age.

Barbara Dettmer

I'm Here

All around me folk are talking
Moving on with such a pace
I've been placed here in the garden
With the sunshine on my face
Someone brings a drink and sandwich
How I wish they'd stop and talk
They just smile and pat me gently
And then quickly off they walk
Is it that I can't contribute?
Now I've reached this ancient stage
Am I totally redundant?
Just because of my great age
Can't they see I'm still a person
With some wisdom still to share
And a heart that still has longings
For someone to show they care
These young people have no notion
Just how quickly time goes past
Before they know it they'll be old too
For halcyon days just do not last
So when you see my isolation
Please give some time to stop and see
That I am still a living being
Oh *please* won't someone talk to me.

Mo Evans

Thoughts of a Geriatric

I sit here by the village pump, a geriatric liability,
According to the local folk my trouble is senility,
But they don't share my memory of years in archaeology
These folk who poke their noses in and call it sociology.
I'm just an old self righteous bum but I am under no one's thumb,
I like folk who are risible and young girls who are kissable,
I have no need to slave these days and though I may have funny
ways
My life's a round of ecstasy, I'm proud of my dexterity;
A frivolous person that is me; of worries I am almost free,
Almost I say because I must admit I've lost that youthful thrust.

Roy Hobbs

The Woman I Remember

She mellowed in time;
Warmed and gently stewed.
Slightly perfumed,
A generous cleavage,
Gentle snowy curls
And a welcoming smile.

She also had
Bent knuckles
And a stoop and
Strangled veins and
Walking pains
And sometimes she forgot
What she ate for lunch.

I prefer to remember
The things that made her
What she was.
A child, a lover,
A mother.

Adrian Cox

Old Man in the Library

He smiled as he shuffled closer
to the radiator's heat;
then fixed his gaze on the distant skyline
and his body into the window seat.
Later he asked for a special book -
when he saw me on my feet -
perhaps to read while waiting
for a friend he hoped to meet.

But silence rules are sacrosanct
in the reference library
so the poor, bent, aged gentleman
could not converse with me
and the local studies section
is kept under lock and key
and the reference librarian
did not happen to be free.

No social chit-chat possible,
to break his lonely stay.
His friendship call unanswered,
in the most unfortunate way.
Meagre warmth his consolation
on a cold winter's day.
And oh my sense of failure
as he rose and limped away!

P Brindle

Old Age

Old age
Rich experience
Golden age
Memories
Wise sage
Faded eyes
Last page
Papery skin
Unbarred cage
Useless body
Helpless rage
Pensioned poverty
Life's destination -
Old age.

Carol Archer

Evening at Hove

The teatime sun still burns my reddened cheeks;
A drowsy peace descends upon the ground;
Sussex reach two-twenty-five for six;
The scorecard seller's call the only sound.

The air conveys a hint of pipe tobacco,
The overpowering warmth a hint of torpor;
A far-off voice says Sussex are too slow,
But on such days, who minds about the score?

I've kept a sandwich for the journey back,
And saved enough to buy a cup of tea;
A book of Browning's verse lies in my pack;
The Independent crossword on my knee.

No longer are there children to be fed;
No mortgage, memos, meetings, telephones;
But bookshops, gardens, painting class, instead,
And pots of tea for two, with buttered scones.

A distant sense of hard reflected white,
A ripple of applause a distant sound;
I close my eyes to rest them from the light;
My paper slips, unwanted, to the ground.

The sun moves on towards a nearby spire
And shadows lengthen near the close of play;
The former glare is rendered bright and clear
In amber glow - the best part of the day.

Michael Irish

The Choice

God how I loathe growing old!
Up to my neck in bloody medicines
Trying to swim to a life hereafter -
I think I'd rather drown.

Today it's the naming of parts.
Can you feel your toes, your fingers?
Are your waterworks OK?
It's too late, you silly young fool.

Take off your earnest life-saver's look -
I've decided to donate my death
To the right to die society
Rather than to medical science.

No more forced feeding
With all those nasty little tablets.
Now I've got my own supply
Of pretty little life takers.

Lewis Coles

Untitled

I wish you were twenty
And I was nineteen,
The sky so blue and the grass so green;
Your hair so dark and your eyes so blue,
All the exciting things we'd do.

But I'm going quite bananas
And I don't know what's the matter;
My hair gets greyer every day
And I keep on getting fatter.

Judith Anne Bedlow

Cloud Bound

The clouds settle on the peeling sill
between the Busy Lizzie and the swept-back curtain

my eyes shuffle in their jaded chair -
they cling to shades of summer
but the outlook grows uncertain

as the clouds mingle with the cool night air
and my mind follows
to await the chill.

Helen Buckingham

Life Goes on

My veil of white made the scene quite unreal
How could people shop and walk down the street
Dogs lift their legs, kids cry and squeal?
The flowers on my lap were heavy with scent,
Some people noticed the car draped with white
But after one glance they were too intent
On their everyday tasks,
It didn't seem right.
How could they do that on this special day?
Surely the world should stop - shout 'Hooray.'

Twenty years on, I drive to the church
The cars go so slowly, at a snail's pace,
The flowers on the coffin quiver and lurch.
I gaze through the window with a set face.
How could people shop and walk down the street
Dogs lift their legs, kids squeal and cry?
Some people noticed the hearse and then stared.
Surely the world should stop - say 'Goodbye.'

May Haywood

Am I Old?

Yes, I know I am old - all the signs are there
Liver spots on my hands and arms, quickly greying hair.

Eyebrows that turn up at the corners
give the impression of Mesistopholes.
A back that won't quite straighten
and frequently aching knees.

Things put away in safe places
that you rarely ever find.
Your circle of friends growing smaller
you feel life is not very kind.

You would like to grow old peacefully,
but your mind continues to roam
on the inevitable spectre
of a residential home.

Yvette M Beaumont

Growing Old

Growing old - examine the words -
    To grow - to expand - to extend.
To keep the mind open for new ideas;
    To be ever ready to bend.
Old - what is old? A dress can be old
    Because it was bought last season.
A tree can be old, a house or a shoe -
    The universe old beyond reason.
'You should grow old gracefully' so they say -
    Relax, ease off, be your age.
And which age should that be? Age inside or out,
    Age public, or private, or sage.
This grey hair means nothing, could dye but I don't.
    My wrinkles, my lines and my sags
All total a life that's been lived and enjoyed;
    So what if my eyes do have bags!
My kids think I'm bright - the older they get
    The more they will talk and discuss.
My grandson says I'm funny and fun
    And he likes me - a really great plus!
You call us oldies and wrinklies and names
    That sound to us old hat.
At your age too, we were the same . . .
    But time takes care of that!
To grow old disgracefully is my true aim.
    To go out with a bang not a sigh.
Remember my smile, remember my laugh
    And make it a 'happy good-bye'.

Edna Leader

Now

Now that your working days are done,
Reflecting on the setting sun
You'll ponder, as the nights draw in
On what you've done and where you've been.

Now that your life is not the same,
And never will be, quite again.
Don't be concerned or feel distressed,
The road you've taken is the best.

Now when the kitchen clock strikes nine,
No more the binds of work and time,
You can relax, and if you choose
Discover all life's different hues.

Now you can learn to speak Chinese!
Or go abroad, if you so please.
Plough through the classics one by one,
But writing verse is much more fun.

Now you can weed and dig and hoe,
There's shrubs to prune and grass to mow,
A hundred jobs will stand in line
You won't know how you'll find the time.

Now you will wonder how you'll 'fare',
The monthly earnings are not there,
But worry not, and be consoled
The DSS has wealth untold!

Now that a year or more's gone by,
You understand much more than I,
I pray I'm right in what I say,
For I (Oh Help!) retire today.

Christine Oddy

Lethargy

That 'get up and go' is retreating
More and more as the years roll along.
I've 'let up' - with no hope of beating
This comatose pull - it's so strong.

The vigour that once was, is fading,
I'm happy to sit in a chair -
The rigour of age all-pervading -
So life's a lethargic affair.

Why don't I do something about it?
If I did, there's the risk I'd repent,
And I won't take the chance - if I flout it -
Of an epitaph '*Got up and went*!'

Doreen Fletcher

Full Circle

I find that
No amount of eulogy
Can now convince me
Old age is other than calamity.
I see no compensation
For physical deterioration -
For failing strength
And lessening speed,
Decreasing breath
Increasing need:
Yet - I would say
Along the way
There lies a plateau of content -
By design or accident
I couldn't know,
But worries quietly recede
Like ebb tide on the shore
And the realisation dawns -
You've seen it all before:
You've seen brash youth's bold eyes
Through nonchalant thick smoke
You've seen the babies grow
At a stroke -
You've seen old age contanker
You've seen worries contort
You've seen the feet of clay you thought not so
And found kindness to be the only light
With hope tight
In it's shadow.

Moyna Broad

So Nice

It is so nice to grow old, with dignified grace,
With greying hair, and a noble face.
Surrounded by those who love and care,
Relaxing in one's favourite chair.

It is so nice to watch the children play,
And tend the garden, on a sunny day.
To listen to music, ever sweet,
With a faithful dog asleep at your feet.

It is so nice to be greeted with a smile,
To be made to feel that life's worthwhile.
And to hear the warming words of cheer,
Poured into that, not quite, deaf ear.

But there comes a time, for every pair,
When the other half, is no longer there.
Perhaps a time when you're left, alone,
With a lifeless room, and a telephone.

And it's not so nice, when it is hard to walk,
And you're bent so low, that you rarely talk.
And people have so much to do,
That they hardly ever notice you.

It is not so nice, when you sit and stare,
When you think of things, no longer there.
And wonder what the future's for,
Now that the past is no more.

Through the glass, the grains of sand,
Ever onward drop.
And I know it is not them,
But 'tis I, will stop.

John Hendeles

Serene Old Age

How is it with you, Death
By almost all abhorred?
Railed at and ill-received,
Friendless, feared, deplored?

Whom almost all would seek to drive away
From their fast-closed yet penetrable door.
But you, in time decreed, must face your task,
And bear the hurt of wrath and odium sore.

So come, friend Death, to me,
Come welcomed to my room;
A long awaited Guest,
Who will bring no gloom.

If, when you come, I cannot speak to you,
Or smile, or raise my hand, that you may know
How welcome to this house your coming is,
I will hang yellow garlands here to show.
You are the last of all my well loved friends.
Open the door. Come through.

Mollie Freeman

The Pensioners of England

Where have all the pensioners gone, now that winter's here?
Slumped in front of TV sets, the fire their only cheer?
Are they holding up the traffic, as across the roads they plod,
Gazing sadly in shop windows, just waiting now for God?

Can they recall the pangs of love, its pleasure and its pain?
Or has their blood turned cold with age, never to quicken again?
Have they 'had it' as the phrase goes, and should gently fade away,
To be seen but seldom heard abroad at the closing of their day?

No! The folk who laughed at Hitler, and bore the brunt of war,
Are still alive and kicking as they were in days of yore.
They are dancing in the ballrooms, and swimming in the pools;
They even crack a joke at times, and play the flaming fool.

They are climbing up the hillsides, hand in hand they tread the lanes,
Their laughter rings out merrily as they rush to board the planes.
And the locals in the winter sun, in Portugal, Greece and Spain
Forget the summer's lager louts, the Pensioners are here again!

So you young ones, learn a lesson; raise your glasses now on high.
'To the pensioners of England; may they laugh until they die!

John Victor Webb

Live Slowly

Breathe slowly and breathe deep
Purest air or foulest smoke,
Drink slowly and drink deep
Finest wine or cheapest coke,
Love slowly and love deep
To feel the joy you need the grief,
Live slowly and live deep
For time is long but life is brief.

Christopher Rosier

Moving on

May hangs the white sheets
Over every hedge and lane.
I also spring clean.

Strawberries and cream.
Is anyone for tennis?
The church clock strikes four.

Bonfires and brambles,
How many days to Christmas?
Rain under tired feet.

Why doesn't it snow?
Eyes scan clouds and sledges rust.
Childhood is long gone.

I wait for the tide
And wonder what happens next.
An off shore wind blows.

Angela Lanyon

When I'm Old

When I'm old, I'll potter in the garden
in a flowered skirt and sunburnt T-shirt.
My old straw hat will catch in the breeze
as I stoop over flowerbeds pulling out weeds.
If the watering can is too heavy,
my grandchildren will fetch it,
while I dig the soil with my trowel,
planting bulbs for spring-time,
thinning and transplanting irises,
grape hyacinths, polyanthus and thyme.

I'll give over worrying about flabby thighs,
eat marmalade for breakfast
and cream with strawberry jam,
red wine casseroles, mushroom pizzas
and chicken served with grated
cheese wrapped up in ham.
I won't be wearing my shocking pink bikini.
My radium-treated area is sensitive to sun
and I don't want melanoma -
as well as carcinoma -
but pottering, doing nothing,
in the summer air will be fun.

While thirty and forty were
just another decade,
fifty, sixty, seventy, eighty, ninety
will be a battle won.

Rosemary Benzing

On the Death of my Father

Detachable, untouchable
nothing and no one to hold.
Observing words pass
tears flow
hymns sing
a transitory smile
infantile in sleep
across the weary lines.

Holding hands in comfort
observing time retraced,
my comfort, his hand.
A final breath no easier than the first,
orphaned in middle age
detachable, untouchable
nothing and no hand to hold.

Roger Bloor

Growing . . . Old?

Wrinkled and hairless and toothless I came,
A thousand moons later I am somewhat the same,
Larger of course but the wrinkles are back;
I still have some hair, but of teeth there's a lack.
But I want you to know I am still *me* within,
I still laugh, I still cry and, hopefully, sin,
I like snazzy sweaters and nice things to eat,
I'd still like to dance if it weren't for my feet.
I have an ambition - to fly into space,
To circle the earth, to touch the moon's face.
Not likely at my age? Oh well, all right,
I'll settle for Concorde - a round-the-world flight.
And listen you youngsters, I am *not* an old bat
A boot or a bag, and I know where I'm at,
I can spell, I can add, divide and subtract,
My body is wrinkled but my brain's still intact.

I love being alive, though not scared to die,
And if when I go my spirit can fly
I may yet touch the moon or Venus or Mars,
And just for a moment be one with the stars!

Eve Craig

Too Late

I have never been one for bemoaning my fate
Accepted my lot
Not giving a jot
Taken life in my stride
Set feelings aside
But more often lately two words keep recurring, *too late*

I dwell on those things I'd intended to do
Have a rewarding career
Sky dive without fear
Write a best seller
Seduce a young feller
Too late says my mind, your young days are through

Those programmes on age just horrify me
Incontinent ladies
Being treated like babies
Unable to stand
Faces quite bland
Is it *too late* to pray please set them free

Be positive Mother, my children will cry
This is only a phase
You don't act your age
You're never depressed
What you need is a rest
Is it *too late* to say I have been living a lie

But let's have a re-think perhaps it's never *too late*
To keep stretching my brain
Write for pleasure *and* gain
Try pastures anew
There *is* plenty to do
I feel quite a lot brighter, must hurry can't wait
Must do it all now before it's *too late*

June Ansell

My Mother

Sarah Meade Thornthwaite 15 November 1895 - 4 December 1988)

She's ninety three, and slipping away: (my mother).
Could be tomorrow, or still be today; (the death of mother).
But the name of the day, or the time of the year
Really doesn't matter, because it's the end of her: (my mother).

Yet soon will be Christmas, she'll be no more: (my mother).
The season joyous, with no emotions raw: (about mother).
So I cry for help at this poignant time: (so sad about mother).
Ecclesiastes answers, and creates this rhyme (when I weep
for mother).

To everything there is a season: (as you well know dear mother).
A time to be born, and this your time to die: (darling mother).
And so I'll try, with all my human reason: (like you dearest mother).
To accept this plan and say goodbye: (to my clever mother).

Weep and laugh, smile and cry,
A day to be born, a day to die.
It's all so simple, such a wonderful plan!
I accept it all; but I shall miss my mam!

Ecclesiastes: Chapter 3 (verses 1 - 8)

Ann Fogg

Plea

I am whole and sane now, I clearly know that
The world is round, the sun shines on the whiskers of a cat
And through the window, there, the sky's revealed.

Trees bend to the wind with blown leaves sealed
Against the rain, rooted to the earth seemingly strong,
To resist the elements through Summer and Winter long.
All is right, everything is in it's place,
But there's a future for me to face
Which is uncertain; that causes my soul to tremble.
Fear of rheumy eyes, ears sealed to sound,
Slavering mouth, legs rooted uncertainly to ground.
Oh, what if I were incontinent,
And my back were doubly bent;
Pained and sore of leg, hand and arm.
I then could remember my youthful charm,
Memories fair of lovers, family and friends,
Journeys undertaken, possessions and fashion trends.
At least there's life within the mind,
Home comforts, food and neighbours kind.
What, though, if my memory failed,
Then within a pain wracked body I were jailed,
With no thoughts or pleasant memories to fill the passing hours.
But timeless terror and nightmares shocking powers.
Would sanity desert me, would I a shambling ruin become,
Would neighbours, friends, loved ones fail to perceive some
Semblance of a man.

Please release me if you can,
To spirit's home, soul's rest,
Rather than be less than best.
Mourn me not, be happy for my heavenly home,
A chance to renew all that I had formerly known.

Roy E Brownlow

To my Children

Don't crucify flowers on crosses of wire,
Don't write cards that will cockle tomorrow
In the rain and the sun which fall on me here.
There is no need for sorrow.
Don't buy marble chippings to cover my bed
Or a slab of white limestone to weigh on my head.

Laugh. Let me *be*.
I have very few needs.
I'd rather you planted
A packet of seeds,
Or a tree,
To grow out of me.

Jean Margaret Peace

The Ebbing Tide

I've climbed the steep hillside of life
And now I'm on the slide
Prepared, after the toil and strife
To sit back for the ride.

My greying hair will colour-streak
My cataract they'll 'do'
My hip will be replaced next week
And with new teeth I'll chew.

The TV there'll be time to see,
Late hours I can keep
And with my card marked OAP
I'll travel on the cheap.

This is what I have waited for,
I'll not sit down and mope,
My pension I will weekly draw
And ask for all the 'dope'.

By 'dope', I mean the gossip 'mun'
Not what dope means to you.
My 'dope' I'll guarantee more fun
And gives a big kick too.

So that's my tale, I'm on the slide
Well on the downward path.
I may be on the ebbing tide
But there's still time to laugh.

If in the 'Green Man' you behold
A cheerful dolled-up tart
The glisters you see are not gold -
That's in her ageing heart.

Joan Poynter

I'll Never be Ready to Say Goodbye

As I get older I have one fear
        and the thought of this produces a tear!
I'll not be afraid when it's time to go,
        but I will be sad - and I feel quite low
                when I think of it.

I'll never be ready to say 'goodbye' -
        not ever to you,
                my girls - my boy.
The most precious gifts, received by me,
        and I want to keep them, eternally!

My joy, my peace, my happiness, my pleasure!
        Most priceless jewels,
                I guard thee in my heart,
                        As treasure.

I won't miss the flowers, the grass, the rain -
        or the white snow flakes.
For as my soul awakes, I'm sure they will be there.
        But I will miss you!

Nor will I miss the skies of blue, the stars, the moon,
        Life's o'er too soon.
                I'll never be ready to say 'goodbye'.

Freda Ball

Farewell to Canutism

Growing old? Oh no, not me.
Youth's a state of mind, you see.
Thinking young means feeling young.
What was that word on the tip of my tongue?

Retired? No, just changing gear.
Do I really want a new career?
More time to write, more time to laze.
How did I live through such hectic days?

These gentler days are full of grace.
But damn those wrinkles on my face.
Clothes still smart, make up right.
Perhaps I should check in a better light.

Active? Oh yes, the joints still supple.
Pass me my pills, it's time for a couple.
No arthritis in the knee.
Chased away by my HRT.

'You're looking well, so fit and slim.'
Thank heavens others' eyes grow dim.
'Such energy, how come you're tireless?
Oh to sit down and turn on the wireless.

'We're having a baby,' my daughter cried.
But 'Gran's not my image,' I feel inside.
'What d'you want your new name to be?'
Well nothing that starts with 'N' or 'G'.

But when the little one was born
No longer were emotions torn.
For this is the benefit of age,
The joy of new life on a virgin page.

Valmai Holt

Irrelevant Age

'You are very old' said the child with unconscious cruelty
but I remembered how an astronomer once told me
that all the heavy metals in the human body
originated from the explosion of a distant star
millions of years ago.

I looked into the child's clear beautiful eyes
seeing the peach bloom skin and shining hair.
Yes, I thought, I'm very old but so are you;
in the time scale of our galaxy
there is little to choose between the two of us.

Ruth Hitchings

Growing Old

A withering image looks back.
Despair is caught like a cold.
Relief at accepting the load
of self-consciousness active again.

Teasing the laws of nature;
Pretending it isn't quite yet
time to stop the pretending,
and settling for second best.

A body listening to unreason
by a mind eager to deceive, is
slow to grasp its meaning, when
the tune is piped unannounced.

Memories repeatedly rosy,
mask what was probably not
reality, now accepted on new terms;
Expected and endured in the ageing.

Then, no watered down impulse of spirit;
The day was seasoned with fun, when
Wisdom tried tipping the scales,
seeming rarely to find the balance.

Crowded days prod the 'moving finger',
Aware now of time's conscious speed.
Wishful of taking that finger, and
pointing it in any other direction.

Resigned to the sand speeding down;
Knowing there's less now to lose.
Booking a seat on the last grain,
leaving a vacuum behind.

Marguerite Haselton

Thicker Knickers

Short, fat and on my way to dust
my comfort is my all,
elastic's gone that held my bust
there's no-one left to maul,
or see the firm foundations
that I wore to hold me in,
I'm liberated now and let
it all hang out, like sin.

My spencers, long johns, Damart all
keep me as warm and snug
as when young ardour made me fall
insensate on the rug,
my wincey nighties cosy me
from top to toe in bed,
more cosseting by far than smalls
that to temptation led.

And so I sit in socks and slacks,
enjoy my comfy clothes,
my shoes are domed, there's tons of room
to wriggle all my toes,
though passion's spent, excitement gone,
there's nothing that I yearn,
let the youngsters carry on,
and churn - and burn - and learn.

Margaret Foreman

On the Death of a Loved One

You seemed to float away on a sea of dark repose
Your eyes to gently fade as mists of death arose

Then you were gone, to think, sense, feel no more
Your bones, flesh, hair, just clothes upon the floor

My heart broke then in desperate disbelief,
Shed each tear as the stricken tree its leaf

Unnumbered legions so have grieved, and cried
Pools of ancient grief in timeless deserts dried.

Shall my tears dry too and memories also fade?
Only as the mountain stream when its course is made.

And now in frozen silence we distil our thoughts of you
The look, the scent, the feel, the being we thought we knew.

I am not with you now in your lonely holocaust,
But you are here with me, touching my soul, burning my heart.

In all the hours and days and years ahead,
Here you will be, here with me.

I look into your picture as you were an age ago,
Your life led on before you to a timeless sunset glow.

Your eyes were still to shine in summer suns unrisen,
Your hair to blow in breezes stirring flowers yet unbidden.

Now your face lies ashen as the powder in the grate,
And you have reached, and known, and passed, the final second
of your fate.

J A Uttley

What Day is it Tomorrow?

Let me get this straight.
What day has it been today?
Monday?
So it's Tuesday tomorrow?
Do I go out on Tuesdays?
Wednesday?
Thursday. Let me write it down.
I go out on Thursday.
And tomorrow is ?
So I don't go out tomorrow
or the next day.

I'm sorry to be such a nuisance
but I'm getting old and forget things.
I'm nearly eighty-four, I think.
I was born in 1904, so that makes me ?
- there you are you see,
getting on for ninety, no wonder.
I was brought up to be on time,
never missed an appointment
and I don't want to start now.
It worries me.

So has it been Tuesday today?
Monday. There I've got it wrong again!
Monday today, so it's Tuesday tomorrow.
Do I go out on Tuesday?
Thursday, I go out on Thursday.
Let me get it down.
Monday, today.
Tuesday, home. Wednesday, home.
Thursday, I go out.
What time do they pick me up on Thursday?

(Found in the words of Mrs M L)

Mary Erricker

State of the Heart

Perilously dentured in a
Province bounded by prescription
Counters and Large Print bookshelves,
We commit the principles of
Forgetfulness to memory.
Here, in the long shadowed sundown
Of illustrious breathing careers,
Where family jowls hang loose and
Noses grow like coral atop
Incredible shrinking bodies,
Our faculties are rakishly
Buttoned out of sequence.

Eyebrows fused like fighting racoons,
Our armies are on the shuffle.
Don't come your new fangle-isms
With us. Chug-Bopalula headsets.
Gateaux blasters and lap top
Jacuzzi's not required.
Urgently required: String bag friendly
Five items or less checkouts.
Smouldering like mattresses
Behind the cheque book doodlers,
We have seen the present and it irks.

Gerry McKee

Marjorie

The postmark wasn't one I knew
It brought me news today of you
I saw again your cheeky grin
The bouncy walk, the joy within your heart -
Your heart of love.

We worked together years ago
And help along this way of woe
Was given to me serene and free
Your faith - a beam of charity - your life
Experience for me.

And hidden in the manner mild
Were fears for your, dear, smitten child
The others fit, supportive, true
To all their mother could impart - her love
For each of them.

The laughter lines are deeper now
The years have etched into your brow
Your character, your life that's past
But still your smile shines forth to glow - and gladden
All around.

My visit sees you on your frame
Your hip repaired - through all the pain
You zim along and persevere
And bounce right back to smile again
For all your friends.

This world's composed of transient things
Your faith shines out - the real smile brings
A happy light into your sphere
A shaft of truth and love is here unfurled -
An aura of peace.

Elizabeth Buckman

Grandaughter

With clear candour of childhood,
She shattered
My dream
Of immortality.

'You have frost in your hair,'
She said.
Then pleaded,
'You will last, won't you?'

Betty Kay

Last Lap

After the menopause
the machine
mysteriously accelerates.
Brakes only partly hold.
The Present
by-passes your brain.
What was that signpost?
Where did you mean to go?
Where is your driving licence?
No use to panic.
Take a firm grip of the wheel
and pray
for the necessary
hard-shoulder.

Dorothy Cowlin

Reflections

Reflecting on my life one day,
both joys and sorrows passed my way.
From childhood through to old age,
the winds of time have certainly changed.
Sand and water, provided fun for the day,
now the complexities of the computer
have come to stay.
The abacus and slide-rule are out of date,
sums these days are easy to calculate.
Press a few buttons here and there,
machinery and gadgets everywhere.
Trams and steam trains, that once were ridden,
surely these are now out driven.
Nobody cared about the world we lived in then,
suddenly we all became the ozones' friend.
Save the elephants, Blue whale and seal
extinct they will become if we do not appeal.
No consideration for other species and races,
we strip the earth of its beautiful places.
Let us stop before complete obliteration,
and throw some light on the turmoil and devastation.
The rays of hope and glory shine, even when in strife,
take a few seconds out of your day, to reflect upon your life.

Nargis Qureshi

Going Home

What shall I do for shadows
when the candlelight is gone,
apart from the grass smocked meadows
in the failing evening sun?

I'll make a fire that's curling
with broken strands of smoke
and call to the wisps that are whirling
from the charcoal blackened oak.

Hear how the chimney answers
as a friend who is always true
and bow to the firefly dancers
on the brightly burning yew.

Now I am done with waiting
as the dream of years is come,
away on the cloud banks skating
to the tryst of the moon and the sun.

Then will the world go under
that the yearly round has made
and roar as it may like thunder,
for it passes me unafraid.

Now is my lone hand taken
and held with a gentle grace
and the dancers will never awaken
in their robes of wind torn lace.

At last I have found my shadows
and the fire is burning low.
I'm gone to the warm green meadows
as I knew them long ago.

Stuart Crabb

No Thanks Methuselah

It was inklings of wrinkles that started
Me thinking crows-feet had a foot in the door,
Would my hair, teeth and I soon be parted?
Bare head and gums at barely two and a half score.

Wrapping once meant gift tags and sticky tape,
Now more often it's up against the cold;
Forget about chic and a waspish shape,
Gracefully's nothing to do with growing old.

John Marshman

Full of Years

I climbed through mist,
Leaving the sunshine of my youth below,
Sometimes I heard childish voices,
Calling me from the valley,
But as the years passed,
They were no more.
Others journeyed with me,
'You're over the top!' one said.
Then it was downhill all the way,
Down to a darker valley with faltering strides.
Now I can see where the path finishes,
Where I will stumble.
Will hands lift me up?
Will I see the light again,
And know my mountaineering was not in vain?

Peter Donaldson

Growing Older

You are not old.
Cease peering at yourself in the mirror
Taking count of the greying hairs,
Tracing each lengthening wrinkle.
Rather look into your heart
Whence the good, red blood flows.

Disillusionment over the years
Seeks to encrust your soul
And hold you fast
With memories of past failures.
Shake them off and,
With a laugh, start life anew.

Make your farewells
And go.
Put foot in front of foot
Until once more
Your path becomes clear,
Maybe to joys and delights undreamed.

Do not look back,
For life will not wait
For those who linger.
By honest endeavour
You shall attain
Your due reward.

E B Steel

The Future of Friends

Two terriers scurry across the fields
Noses deep in long grass that is their jungle.
Tails wag joyfully, brown eyes gleam with delight,
Confident of a good day, no fears of the future.

Your happiness is in our hands, our responsibility,
You own our hearts, we provide your well-being.
Your life span is almost predictable.
But what of us, your keepers? There is no such prediction.

How to explain if our limbs cannot walk you as before?
Who will soothe your puzzlement if we are no longer here,
Comprehend your rituals, the routines we gave you,
When the longing in your eyes is your only speech.

We mould your lives to our whims and to yours,
We pride ourselves on your trust, your loyalty,
We revel in your unquestioning friendship,
So there is a price to pay, a prayer for you.

That you go first, dear friends,
Carefree and untroubled to the end,
Unaware we are bereft of your company
Talking to your photographs.

Pat Austin Stone

This Retiring Life

Yesterday I said Goodbye. I'd come to the end
Of a part of my life.
Cosy slippers, fireside chair, dreaming away each day -
Was this for me?
No. Today is freedom; the future stretches ahead
Like an ever expanding ray of sunshine,
Pulling me in its wake, urging me
To new excitements.
No more the bonds which kept me
Harnessed to life's achievements.
Today, new forces tingle through my being,
Seducing me to a fulfilment
Of dreams long dreamed.
Today, the hours too short
For all my new beginnings.
Energy, in its manifold guises, pulsates in my veins.
Yet peace, like a halo protecting me,
Allows time to reflect, to appreciate
The calmness bestowed by decades
Of experience.
How good, this retiring life.

Ruth Chapman

Keep on Knocking

'Keep on knocking, but you can't come in.'
This glass is your shield
and protector
from those who would claw
your trusting curious eyes
out of simple boredom.

Each day you come here
stroking, tapping, feeling
as thoroughly
as any blind Braille reader.
But the surface is smooth, as barren
as the inside of your head.
You will never gain admittance unless
you scream and strike
and tear flesh,
unless you horde, mouse-like,
your daily ration:
bright pellets
to be downed in the sad child's orgy
borne of true loneliness.

Keep on knocking, who knows
some day another
may, in secret, come this far
may tap back
in a code you will recognise,
breaking the glass that separates
your two worlds.

Jocelyn M Britcher

Old Man's Memories

Old men's dreams run through the head:
Such fantasies and fancies bred!
Elusive pictures in the mind
With memories all ill-defined.

A thrush upon a leafless bough
Against a sunset sky on fire:
A song so piercing sweet, yet now
The echoes stir but small desire.

Clear eyes that smiled with sweet desire,
And tumbled hair all soft and dark:
Two minds and hearts so set afire . . .
Now, long dead embers raise no spark.

Two peaches on a slender tree:
A rosebud in the grass below . . .
But where and when reality?
The picture faded long ago.

Old men's dreams are vague and blurred,
Emotions scarcely to be stirred.
Gone the brightness: gone the day . . .
So long ago: so far away.

Austin Shorney

Growing Old

I have reached that
Blessed state of
Freedom.
Doing as I please
Switching off
The Telly
Eating rubbish
Drinking sherry.

Being ill in India
But seeing the Taj.
Sleeping out
In Africa.
Collecting grandchildren
I shall not see
Reach maturity.

Josephine Bromley

Growing Old

What of this business, growing old?
so many stories have been told,
much is written, much is said,
computers have their data fed,
the medical may diagnose,
philosophers their mind disclose,
this universal ailment,
no one born, from this exempt;
but who can best explain this state?
surely those to graduate,
and who can best my years define?
experience of life that's mine,
a task too great to analyse
or in these lines to summarise,
as I've achieved ten and threescore,
and some are blessed with years more,
is there advice that I can give
for those who would a lifetime live?
don't pay much heed to aches and pains
a mind of wealth old age retains,
but should we think ourselves as old?
'tis as we feel, not as we're told,
so many things there are to do
each day reveals a prospect new,
think not these years a sad decline
the will for good, will mind refine,
tho' looking back in lots of ways,
whate'er we think of 'good old days',
the change of fashion, style, and trend,
of changing things, there'll be no end,
but one thing changeless, I can name -
true love of heart, can be the same!

Arthur George Carter

A Rest Home (They Say)

Eyes so big you wouldn't believe
They were starving - begging love or
Hate - any emotion please the invisible sign reads.

They sit in lines
As birds waiting to peck - yet
Rain doesn't come, sun doesn't shine.

Devoid of emotion? No.
Below the layers of age
They await the ultimate catharsis.

The wheel of fortune?
Did they say you'd finally be reminded
Of the childhood you don't really remember?

Spoon fed in a babygrow.
Now? The difference being suit and tie.
So? Life - cyclic - life.

All innocence in eyes so big.
They respond -
I thought there'd be
An eternal kiss!

Marian Thomas